BLUE-RIBBON COOKBOOK

FIRST EDITION

BLUE-RIBBON COOKBOOK

FIRST EDITION

Judy Harrold, C.H.E.
Editor

State Fair Books
Indianapolis, Indiana
1992

Recipes provided by Ball Premium Fair Awards winners have been judged to be the best in their class by their respective state and county fair officials. Ball Corporation has evaluated the canned recipes for correct processing methods; however, such recipes have not been tested by Ball Corporation for quality or safety. Only those recipes submitted by Ball Corporation have been tested by Ball for quality and safety.

Front-cover photo features Apricot-Pineapple Banana Nut Bread and Citrus Spiced Carrots.

All inquiries should be addressed to:
BALL BLUE-RIBBON COOKBOOK
c/o State Fair Books
P. O. Box 30225
Indianapolis, IN 46230-0225

Printed in the United States of America

CONTENTS

PREFACE

Ball Corporation is steeped in family heritage and a commitment to excellence. Its history started before the turn of the century and continues to wind into the future. The five brothers who worked side by side to launch their business over one hundred years ago, the family members who continue to be a part of Ball Corporation today, and the devoted employees who have worked for Ball over the years have seen the company take many turns and changing paths to reach its present destination. But through the years, one constant has remained a cornerstone of the company—Ball home canning jars.

During the early 1900s the acceptance of home canned foods carried Ball Corporation—then Ball Brothers Glass Manufacturing Company—to the forefront of the fruit jar business. At the same time, the concern Ball gave to the proper use of their product led to the creation of what we know today as the *Ball Blue Book*. The focus of the *Ball Blue Book* was then, and is today, to ensure safety, quality and the economical preparation of home canned foods.

The original recipes were developed in the kitchen of George A. Ball and his wife, Frances Woodworth Ball. They created their own recipes and gathered many from family and friends. Over the years, Ball has tested hundreds of recipes, developing safe, up-to-date guidelines. Today, Ball is considered an authority on home canning and maintains its position as a major manufacturer of home canning products.

What the Ball family did not know those many years ago was the important role "that collection of recipes" would play in thousands of homes across America even today. The recipes they shared have become a mainstay for home canning enthusiasts and have served to inspire creativity in food preservation.

To encourage home canning as a part of quality living and to reward those dedicated to its art, Ball Corporation developed a program to honor excellence in food preservation. Every year, for more than twenty years, county and state fairs across the nation have selected the top entrants to receive the highest honor of a Ball first place award. Thousands of awards have been presented to individuals whose exhibits best represent quality home canned foods prepared from recipes in the *Ball Blue Book* and for original recipes based on sound canning practices.

The *Ball Blue-Ribbon Cookbook, First Edition*, is a compilation of the best of the blue ribbon recipes. You will find a wide variety of recipes, ranging from Apple Cinnamon Jelly to Zucchini Bread and Butter Pickles, selected from the very program that honors excellence. We are also sharing some of our favorite recipes developed in the Ball Test Kitchen.

To demonstrate the versatility and usefulness of home canned foods, we have included recipes using these foods in prepared dishes. You will enjoy specialities such as Baked Asparagus with Almond-Cheese Sauce, Chicken Cacciatore, Maple Apple Tea Ring, and Chocolate Raspberry Dream Cake, along with many more recipes using canned fruits, vegetables, jams and jellies, and pickles and relishes.

As always, we feel the best home canned foods start with up-to-date guidelines. To instruct the first time canner and to review with the experienced canner, we have provided all of the necessary canning basics needed to prepare the home canned recipes in this cookbook.

With the completion of this cookbook, we come to the end of yet another new path. Along the way, many friends were made and wonderful ideas exchanged—all of which makes for a short journey. We are delighted with the result of our effort and confident that it will become a tradition of excellence.

It is our pleasure to honor the blue ribbon winners who share our dedication to quality living. The *Ball Blue-Ribbon Cookbook* will be a valuable tool in our educational efforts to promote safe food preservation.

INTRODUCTION

The award winning recipes in this book are based on current home canning guidelines. All home canners, new or experienced, should read the general guidelines for home canning before starting any canning project. Successful home canning begins with up-to-date guidelines.

GENERAL GUIDELINES
Your canning should start with garden fresh fruits and vegetables, the right equipment, and a time-proven method for success. The two basic methods of canning are:

■ the pressure canner, which superheats low acid foods and kills harmful bacteria

■ the boiling water bath method, which processes high acid foods at high heat and destroys bacteria, enzymes, molds, and yeasts

Check Your Jars and Lids
Use only home canning jars, not jars in which commercial food has been sold (such as mayonnaise or peanut butter jars). Visually examine jars and sealing surfaces for nicks, cracks, and sharp edges that can ruin the finished seal. Jars are reusable if they are in good condition. Remember, however, that processing times differ according to the size of the container. It is recommended to use only the size jar specified in the recipe.

Use only the two-piece vacuum cap. The set consists of a flat metal lid with a flanged edge, the underside of which has a rubber-like sealing compound, and a threaded metal screw band that fits over the rim of the jar to hold the lid in place.

The manufacturer's directions should be followed to use this closure.

Lids are not reusable because the sealing compound will not form a seal twice.

Bands are reusable if in a reasonable, unwarped, unrusted condition.

Fill the Jars
■ Wash and rinse lids and bands.

■ Place lids in a small saucepan of water, bring water to a simmer and remove from heat. **Do not boil.**

■ Prepare the checked-over jars by washing them in hot soapy water. Rinse well. Then soak the jars in hot water, keeping the water hot until the jars are removed to be filled with food. Jars in which food will be processed for less than 10 minutes must be sterilized. To sterilize jars before filling, place them right side up on the rack in a boiling water bath canner. Fill the canner and jars with hot (not boiling) water to one inch above jar tops. Boil 10 minutes at altitudes of less than 1,000 feet above sea level. At higher elevations, boil one additional minute for each additional 1,000 foot elevation. Allow jars to remain in hot water until ready to use. Remove one at a time as needed. Jars to be processed for 10 minutes and longer do not need to be sterilized, but must be kept hot until ready to be filled. A dishwasher may also be used to wash the jars and keep them warm, but cannot be used to sterilize jars. (Do not use an oven to warm the jars, as it may cause them to break.)

■ Carefully fill the hot jars one at a time and place them in the canner while they are still hot to help prevent breakage. To reduce the possibility of jar breakage: never pour boiling water or hot food into a room temperature jar; never place a room temperature jar into boiling water; and never place a hot processed jar on a cool or wet surface.

To further reduce jar breakage, always use non-metallic utensils when filling the jars, releasing air bubbles, or removing food from the jars. Never use metal knives to release air bubbles, and never use steel wool to clean the jars. Always be careful when working with boiling liquids and filling the jars with hot foods.

■ Leave the correct amount of headspace (air space between the top of the jar and top level of the food). In general, headspace is one inch for vegetables, meats, poultry, seafoods and soups; ½ inch for fruits, tomatoes and sauerkraut; ¼ inch for jellies and other semi-soft spreads, and pickles, relishes and juices.

■ Release trapped air bubbles after filling jars by running a non-metallic spatula around the inside of each jar next to the glass.

■ Wipe jar rim clean. The lid is placed over the mouth of the jar so that the sealing compound rests on the rim. Screw the band down firmly so that it is hand tight. Do not use a jar wrench or other device to tighten the screw band.

During processing, there is enough "give" in the lid to allow air to exhaust from the jar. The screw band should not be tightened or loosened after processing. As the jar cools, a vacuum inside the jar will pull the lid down in the center so that it is slightly concave. A slight pinging sound may be heard as the seal is formed. After 12 to 24 hours, the jars will be thoroughly cooled. When jars are completely cooled, remove screw bands and check the seal. The center of the lid should have been pulled down by a vacuum and will be slightly concave. Wash outside jar surface. Store properly sealed jar in a cool, dry, dark place.

To open, use a can opener to release the vacuum, then lift off lid. Discard lid; it is not reusable.

Process the Filled Jars

■ In handling the jars, care should be taken that they do not crack or break due to sudden changes of temperature.

■ Place the filled jars in the canner one at a time, as you fill them and while they are still hot.

■ Be sure to use a pressure canner for all vegetables, meats, poultry, seafoods and soups. Boiling water bath canning is only for fruits, tomatoes, pickles, jellies and semi-soft spreads, and juices.

■ For the boiling water bath method, place raw packed jars in hot water in canner and place hot packed jars in simmering water in canner. Add boiling water if necessary to bring the water one to two inches over the tops of jars. Return to a full boil before you begin to count processing time.

■ For the pressure canning method, fill bottom of canner with two to three inches of hot water and add filled jars. Close canner, place over heat, and allow steam to vent steadily for 10 minutes. If for any reason the pressure should drop during processing, the entire processing time must be repeated.

■ Follow your recipe's required processing time and temperature. Do not allow temperature or pressure to fluctuate during processing time. (In high altitude areas, make the necessary changes in processing time or pressure according to the altitude charts.)

■ When processing time is complete, remove jars with a jar lifter. Place on clean, dry cloths or wooden board. Do not place jars on a cool or wet surface. (Wait 10 minutes after opening canner to remove jars when using a pressure canner.) Let your canned hot food cool naturally and out of drafts. Do not retighten bands. (Do not place pressure canner under running water to cool.)

■ After the jars have cooled, test the seal on each jar by pressing down on the center of the lid. If the lid does not push down, it is sealed. If the lid pushes down and springs back up, it has not sealed and the food should be fully reprocessed or refrigerated immediately. Remove bands and store the canned food in a cool, dry, dark place for up to one year.

HIGH ACID FOODS

Acid foods are those that contain natural acid. Each food is different, and different varieties of the same food may vary in acidity. Most fruits, tomatoes, jellies and semi-soft spreads, and pickles are high acid foods. They may be canned in a boiling water bath canner, which kills any harmful microorganisms at 212°F. (Bacteria do not thrive in acid foods.) High acid foods can be hot packed or raw packed, the main difference being that the raw or cold pack is preferred for fragile foods and the hot pack is preferred for foods that tend to float or rise to the top of the jar after processing.

Food that is hot packed should be precooked in water, in a syrup, or in the juice that is extracted. After food is packed into the jar, it should be covered with the hot cooking liquid. Fruit canned without sweetening is always hot packed.

If food is to be raw packed, the food is placed into the jar while it is raw. It should be packed firmly but should not be crushed. After packing, boiling syrup, juice or water is added to foods that require additional liquid.

Fruits

Some fruits such as apples, apricots, pears, and peaches tend to darken while being canned. This can be counteracted by soaking the fruit in an anti-darkening solution. When using a commercial product, follow manufacturer's instructions. If a commercial fruit preserver is not used, soak fruit in a solution of 2 tablespoons each of salt and white distilled vinegar and 1 gallon of water. Do not leave fruit soaking longer than 20 minutes. Rinse fruit thoroughly before packing. Fruits are always packed in liquid (unsweetened fruit juice or syrup), usually 1 to 1½ cups per quart. To make syrup, sugar is combined with water or fruit juice and cooked until sugar dissolves. Keep syrup hot until needed, but not cooked down completely.

SYRUPS FOR CANNING

Type of Syrup	Sugar	Water	Yield
Extra light	1 cup	4 cups	4½ cups
Light	2 cups	4 cups	5 cups
Medium	3 cups	4 cups	5½ cups
Heavy	4¾ cups	4 cups	6½ cups

Medium with Corn Syrup: Use 1½ cups sugar, 1 cup corn syrup to 3 cups liquid.
Medium with Honey: Use 1 cup sugar, 1 cup honey to 4 cups liquid.

Jellies and Semi-Soft Spreads

All jellies must be processed for 5 minutes in a boiling water bath canner. Because of the short processing time, it is necessary to sterilize the jars and keep them hot before using.

Jelly is made from fruit juice and contains no fruit pulp. To extract the juice from hard fruits (apples, pears, etc.), cover the fruit with water; for soft fruits (berries, grapes, etc.), add just enough water to prevent scorching. Cook fruits until they are tender and the natural juices begin to flow. Remove from heat. Strain juice through a damp jelly bag or cheesecloth. Allow the fruit to drain until all the juice is extracted (this may take several hours). Do not squeeze the bag as this will cause the jelly to be cloudy. Follow jelly recipe for preparation.

Jams, preserves, conserves, marmalades, and butters are processed for 10 minutes or more; processing times will vary depending on the recipe. It is not necessary to sterilize the jars before using; however, the jars should be heated in water and kept in hot water until they are used. When preparing the fruit for these spreads, crush or chop according to recipe directions. Do not crush or chop fruit too fine as this will add too much liquid and too much fruit for a good gel. Follow recipe directions for cooking and processing times.

All jellies and semi-soft spreads must be processed in a boiling water bath canner. It is no longer recommended to use the open kettle method or paraffin when sealing jars.

NOTE: Use only the type of pectin called

for in the recipe. Powdered pectin and liquid pectin are not interchangeable. Making a substitution may prevent the recipe from gelling.

Pickles and Relishes

Pickles refer not only to cucumbers, but to any vegetable, fruit or meat prepared by a pickling process. The boiling water bath canner is the processing method used, and each pickle and relish recipe has individual processing requirements. Begin counting processing time as soon as jars are placed in canner for brined pickles and fresh-pack dills. For all other pickles, return water in canner to a full boil before starting to count processing time.

Do not use utensils of zinc, iron, brass, aluminum, copper, galvanized metal or enamelware with chips or cracks when preparing brine. For fermented pickles, use a crock, stone jar, unchipped enameled pot, glass jar or hardwood kegs with enamel, glass or paraffin lining plus a heavy lid.

Always use vinegar of a 5% acidity strength to ensure the proper acid level of pickled products. Either white, distilled vinegar or cider vinegar can be used.

LOW ACID FOODS

Low acids are foods that contain very little natural acid. Low acid foods, which include vegetables, meats, poultry, seafood and soups, are mostly hot packed. Mixed canned foods that might contain part low acids (such as corn) and part acids (such as tomatoes) should be treated as low acids. To ensure that all potentially harmful bacteria are killed, low acid foods must be processed a set length of time in a pressure canner at 240°F (10 pounds pressure at sea level). As a precaution, after canning, low acid foods should be boiled for 15 minutes before serving or even tasting.

The manufacturer's directions should be followed for your own pressure canner. If using a dial gauge canner, have the gauge checked for accuracy on an annual basis.

After the canner is filled with jars and the lid is adjusted in place, allow steam to vent from the pressure canner for 10 minutes before adjusting the weight and counting the processing time. And remember to let the canner cool naturally after processing. Do not open the lid until the pressure is reduced to 0 pounds.

Adjustments for Altitude

Because air is thinner at higher altitudes, both pressures and boiling points are affected. That means that with both the boiling water bath and the pressure canner methods, adjustments in processing must be made. With the boiling water method, additional processing time must be allowed. With the pressure canner method, additional pressure is required. The altitude charts show the requirements for both methods at various altitudes.

ALTITUDE CHART FOR WATER BATH CANNER

In high altitude areas, processing times for the boiling water bath canner differ from the times given in this cookbook. Compensations for areas above 1,000 feet are listed below:

Altitude, Feet	Increase Processing Time
1,001 - 3,000	5 minutes
3,001 - 6,000	10 minutes
6,001 - 8,000	15 minutes
8,001 - 10,000	20 minutes

ALTITUDE CHART FOR PRESSURE CANNER

Pressure levels for the pressure canner are different for high altitude areas. Compensations for areas above 1,000 feet are:

Altitude, Feet	Dial Gauge	Weighted Gauge
0 - 1,000	10	10
1,001 - 2,000	11	15
2,001 - 4,000	12	15
4,001 - 6,000	13	15
6,001 - 8,000	14	15
8,001 - 10,000	15	15

VEGETABLES

CANNED ASPARAGUS 14 ■ Baked Asparagus with Almond-Cheese Sauce 15 ■ Grilled Asparagus 15 ■ Cream of Asparagus Soup 16 ■ CANNED GREEN BEANS 17 ■ Swiss-Style Green Beans 18 ■ Green Bean Casserole 18 ■ Green Bean Bundles 19 ■ Barbecued Green Beans 19 ■ Green Beans Salad 20 ■ Cheesy Green Bean Casserole 20 ■ Vegetable Medley 21 ■ CANNED KIDNEY BEANS 21 ■ Macaroni Vegetable Salad 22 ■ CANNED BABY BEETS 23 ■ Harvard Beets 24 ■ Marinated Beet Salad 24 ■ Sweet-and-Sour Beets 25 ■ CANNED CARROTS 25 ■ Carrot Casserole 26 ■ Carrot Ring 27 ■ Citrus Spiced Carrots 27 ■ CANNED SUMMER SQUASH 28 ■ Cream of Zucchini Soup 29 ■ Squash Delight Casserole 29 ■ CANNED YAMS 30 ■ Candied Yams 31 ■ CANNED MIXED VEGETABLES 32 ■ LUANNE'S CHILI 33

VEGETABLES

Canned Asparagus

4 pounds asparagus (freshly
   picked finger-size stalks)
Salt (optional)

Prepare home canning jars and lids according to manufacturer's instructions.

Wash asparagus thoroughly. Remove scales and trim off tough ends of stalks. Cut asparagus into lengths that will fit upright in pint jars, leaving one-inch headspace. Pack asparagus into hot jars (stem end at bottom of jar). Add ½ teaspoon salt to each pint, if desired. Cover with boiling water, leaving one-inch headspace. Remove air bubbles with a non-metallic spatula. Adjust caps.

Process pints 30 minutes at 10 pounds pressure in a pressure canner.

Yield: about 8 pints

NOTE: Leftover pieces of asparagus may be canned to use in soup.

Cynthia Westermier, Arcadia, Oklahoma (State Fair of Oklahoma, Oklahoma City, Oklahoma)

Baked Asparagus with Almond-Cheese Sauce

1 quart (4 cups) Canned Asparagus,
   drained
¼ cup (½ stick) butter or margarine
½ cup small bread cubes
2 tablespoons all-purpose flour
1 cup milk
1 cup shredded sharp cheddar cheese
½ cup slivered almonds, toasted
Salt and pepper to taste

Preheat oven to 350°F.

Arrange asparagus in a greased shallow baking dish; set aside. Melt butter or margarine in a saucepan. Combine 2 tablespoons melted butter with bread cubes, mixing well to coat; set aside. Blend flour into remaining butter in saucepan. Add milk to flour and butter mixture; cook and stir until thickened. Add cheese, almonds, salt, and pepper to mixture in saucepan; stir until cheese melts. Pour sauce over asparagus in baking dish. Sprinkle buttered bread cubes over top.

Bake at 350°F about 20 minutes.

Yield: 4 servings

*Terry Swann, Selbyville, Delaware
(Delaware State Fair, Harrington,
Delaware)*

Grilled Asparagus

1½ cups bread crumbs
½ cup grated cheese
1 tablespoon butter or margarine, melted
⅛ teaspoon salt (or to taste)
⅛ teaspoon pepper (or to taste)
⅛ teaspoon paprika (or to taste)
1¼ pints (2½ cups) Canned Asparagus,
   drained
Parsley and pimientos (for garnish)
No-stick vegetable cooking spray

Spray a broiler pan with no-stick cooking spray; set aside. Combine bread crumbs, cheese, and butter or margarine; mix well. Add salt, pepper, and paprika; mix well. Roll asparagus in bread-crumb mixture and arrange on broiler pan. Broil four to six inches from source of heat until heated through, turning frequently to brown evenly. Serve on a hot platter, garnished with parsley and pimientos.

Yield: 6 servings

*Irene Robison, Woodstock, Maryland
(Maryland State Fair, Timonium,
Maryland)*

Cream of Asparagus Soup

1 pint (2 cups) Canned Asparagus
2 tablespoons butter or margarine
2 tablespoons flour
¼ teaspoon onion powder
Salt and pepper to taste
3 cups milk or cream
½ cup processed cheese spread

Drain asparagus, reserving liquid. Cut off asparagus tips and combine with some of the reserved liquid in a saucepan; boil 15 minutes, then set aside. Put remaining pieces of asparagus in blender container and purée; add some of the reserved liquid, if necessary.

Melt butter or margarine in a medium saucepan. Blend in flour, onion powder, salt, and pepper; add puréed asparagus and milk. Cook, stirring occasionally, until mixture comes to a boil (about 5 minutes). Add cheese and continue cooking just until cheese melts. Watch carefully so mixture does not scorch.

To serve, drain asparagus tips and divide evenly among soup bowls. Pour hot soup over tips.

Yield: 4 to 6 servings

NOTE: This is a nice, easy dish when you are hungry for a bowl of soup on a cold winter day, and it doesn't take long to prepare.

Paula G. Webb, Wichita, Kansas (Kansas State Fair, Hutchinson, Kansas)

Canned Green Beans

14 pounds green beans (young,
    tender beans with no bulges)
Salt (optional)

Prepare home canning jars and lids according to manufacturer's instructions.

Wash beans thoroughly, rinsing three times. Remove stems, ends, and strings; break beans into one-inch pieces. Bring 4 cups water to a boil in a three-quart saucepan. Add beans to boiling water and boil 5 minutes.

Pack hot beans into hot quart jars, leaving one-inch headspace. Cover with water from saucepan or with fresh boiling water. Add 1 teaspoon salt to each quart, if desired. Remove air bubbles with a non-metallic spatula. Adjust caps.

Process quarts 25 minutes at 10 pounds pressure in a pressure canner.

Yield: about 7 quarts

Barbara Kellogg, Coushatta, Louisiana (Red River Parish Fair, Coushatta, Louisiana)

Swiss-Style Green Beans

¼ cup (½ stick) butter or margarine,
  melted
2 tablespoons flour
1 teaspoon salt
1 teaspoon sugar
¼ teaspoon pepper
1 teaspoon minced onion
1 cup dairy sour cream
1 quart (4 cups) Canned Green Beans,
  drained
2 cups grated Swiss cheese
½ cup cracker crumbs

Preheat oven to 350°F.

In a large saucepan, combine 2 tablespoons of the butter or margarine with flour, salt, sugar, pepper, and onion; mix well. Add sour cream and cook over medium heat, stirring constantly, until mixture thickens. Add green beans and mix well. Spoon mixture into a greased two-quart casserole dish. Sprinkle cheese over beans; top with cracker crumbs. Drizzle remaining butter over cracker crumbs.

Bake at 350°F for 30 to 35 minutes or until bubbly.

Yield: 6 servings

*Pauline Jenkins, Bakersfield, California
(Kern County Fair, Bakersfield, California)*

Green Bean Casserole

1 quart (4 cups) Canned Green Beans,
  drained
1 (10¾ ounce) can cream of mushroom
  soup
1 (2½ ounce) jar sliced mushrooms,
  drained (optional)
1 (2 ounce) jar sliced pimientos, drained
1 (2.8 ounce) can French-fried onions
  (optional)

Preheat oven to 350°F.

Combine green beans, soup, mushrooms, and pimientos; mix well. Spoon mixture into a 1½-quart baking dish.

Bake at 350°F for 30 minutes. If desired, sprinkle French-fried onions over top of casserole for the last 5 minutes of baking.

Yield: 6 to 8 servings

NOTE: This recipe is simple, delicious, and nutritious, and it's not time-consuming to prepare.

*Eva M. Hudson, Hanna City, Illinois
(Heart of Illinois Fair, Peoria, Illinois)*

Green Bean Bundles

8 green onions
2 pints (4 cups) Canned Green Beans,
    drained (use whole beans)
8 slices bacon
Worcestershire sauce (to taste)
No-stick vegetable cooking spray

Preheat oven to 350°F. Spray a baking pan with no-stick cooking spray; set aside.

Wash and trim onions. Depending on size of beans, group 6 or 8 beans around 1 green onion, then wrap a slice of bacon around the "bean bundle." Place bean bundle on prepared baking pan with seam side of bacon down. Sprinkle 3 or 4 drops of Worcestershire sauce on bean bundle. Repeat with remaining onions, beans, and bacon slices.

Bake at 350°F for 20 minutes or until bacon is done.

Yield: 8 servings

NOTE: Other spices or sauces such as soy sauce can be substituted according to taste. Bean bundles should not be dry.

*Carolyn Bice, Haynesville, Louisiana
(Claiborne Parish Fair, Haynesville,
Louisiana)*

Barbecued Green Beans

4 slices bacon, finely chopped
¼ cup chopped onion
½ cup ketchup
¼ cup brown sugar
1 tablespoon Worcestershire sauce
1 quart (4 cups) Canned Green Beans,
    drained

Preheat oven to 350°F.

Combine bacon and onion in a skillet; cook until browned. Add ketchup, brown sugar, and Worcestershire sauce; simmer 2 minutes. Place green beans in a 1½-quart casserole. Pour bacon mixture over beans; do not stir.

Bake at 350°F for 20 minutes.

Yield: 4 servings

*Warren L. Knudtson, Las Vegas, Nevada
(Las Vegas Jaycees State Fair, Las Vegas,
Nevada)*

Green Beans Salad

1 quart (4 cups) Canned Green Beans,
  drained
1 pint (2 cups) Canned Kidney Beans,
  drained
1 pint (2 cups) canned lima beans,
  drained
1 pint (2 cups) canned green peas, drained
1½ cups sugar
1 cup vinegar
2 tablespoons water
½ cup vegetable oil

Combine all beans and peas in a large mixing bowl. Mix sugar, vinegar, water, and oil; pour over vegetables. Refrigerate overnight.

Yield: 9 to 12 servings

Carrie Carr, Bluff City, Tennessee (Appalachian Fair Association, Gray, Tennessee)

Cheesy Green Bean Casserole

2 teaspoons plus 2 tablespoons butter or
  margarine, divided
1 teaspoon minced onion
1 tablespoon flour
½ teaspoon salt
⅛ teaspoon pepper
1 cup dairy sour cream
1 quart (4 cups) Canned Green Beans
1 (2½ ounce) jar mushrooms, drained
  (optional)
2 cups grated Swiss or Monterey Jack
  cheese
2 cups fresh bread crumbs

Preheat oven to 350°F. Grease a 1½- to 2-quart baking dish; set aside.

Melt 2 teaspoons butter or margarine in a saucepan or skillet; add onion and sauté until transparent. Stir in flour, salt, pepper, and sour cream; cook, stirring constantly, until sauce bubbles (do not boil). Remove from heat.

Heat beans in their own liquid; drain. Combine beans, mushrooms, and sour cream sauce; spoon mixture into greased baking dish. Top with grated cheese. Combine bread crumbs and 2 tablespoons melted butter; sprinkle over cheese.

Bake uncovered at 350°F for 20 minutes or until heated through.

Yield: 8 servings

NOTE: This is good served with baked chicken. The casserole can be assembled ahead of time and refrigerated (add 30 minutes to baking time).

Taffy Benson, Colfax, Wisconsin (Northern Wisconsin State Fair, Chippewa Falls, Wisconsin)

Vegetable Medley

1 pint (2 cups) Canned Green Beans, drained (use tiny whole beans)
1 pint (2 cups) canned tiny English sweet peas, drained
1 pint (2 cups) canned whole kernel corn, drained
1 large sweet onion, chopped
1 large sweet green pepper, chopped
2 stalks celery, chopped
1 (4 ounce) jar pimientos, drained and chopped
¾ cup vinegar
¾ cup sugar
¾ cup corn oil

Combine drained vegetables in a salad bowl. Add onion, green pepper, celery, and pimientos. Combine vinegar, sugar, and oil; pour over vegetables. Refrigerate several hours before serving.

Yield: 8 servings

NOTE: This dish keeps well refrigerated.

Edna Alexander, Harrison, Arkansas
(Northwest Arkansas District Fair,
Harrison, Arkansas)

Canned Kidney Beans

6 pounds dried kidney beans
Salt (optional)

Cover beans with cold water; let stand 12 to 18 hours in a cool place.

Prepare home canning jars and lids according to manufacturer's instructions.

Boil beans 30 minutes. Pack hot beans into hot jars, leaving one-inch headspace. Add ½ teaspoon salt to each pint, if desired. Cover with boiling water, leaving one-inch headspace. Remove air bubbles with a non-metallic spatula. Adjust caps.

Process pints 1 hour and 15 minutes at 10 pounds pressure in a pressure canner.

Yield: about 6 pints

Ball Recipe

Macaroni Vegetable Salad

1 pint (2 cups) Canned Kidney Beans,
   drained
Vinegar
1 (8 ounce) package rotini macaroni,
   cooked according to package directions
1 pint (2 cups) Canned Green Beans,
   drained
1 (10 ounce) package frozen peas, thawed
1 (2 ounce) jar pimientos, drained and
   chopped
1 small onion, chopped
1 cup chopped celery
½ cup chopped sweet green pepper
2 cups mayonnaise
1 cup half-and-half
1 teaspoon prepared mustard
½ cup sugar

Place kidney beans in a small bowl; cover
with vinegar. Let beans stand 1 hour, then
drain. Combine kidney beans with
macaroni, green beans, peas, pimientos,
onion, celery, and green pepper. In a small
bowl, mix mayonnaise, half-and-half,
mustard, and sugar. Pour dressing over
salad and mix lightly. Chill before serving.

Yield: about 12 servings

NOTE: This makes a large salad—good to
take to pot-luck dinners.

*Norma Souser, Otis, Colorado (Washington
County Fair, Akron, Colorado)*

Canned Baby Beets

12 pounds beets (1 to 2 inches in
   diameter)
Salt (optional)

Prepare home canning jars and
lids according to manufacturer's
instructions.

Pick beets just before processing.
Wash beets thoroughly in cold
water. Cut off tops, leaving 1 to
1½ inches of the stem; do not cut
off roots. Rinse beets again. Place
beets in a saucepan and cover with
cold water. Bring to a rapid boil
and cook until skins will come off
easily. Remove skins and trim off
stems and roots; leave beets whole.
Rinse beets with hot water.

Dice three or four beets and place
in a saucepan; cover with two
inches of water and bring to a
boil. Pack whole beets into hot
pint jars, leaving one-inch
headspace. Strain liquid from
diced beets and pour over beets in
jars, leaving one-inch headspace.
Add ½ teaspoon salt to each pint,
if desired. Remove air bubbles
with a non-metallic spatula.
Adjust caps.

Process pints 30 minutes at 10
pounds pressure in a pressure
canner.

Yield: about 7 pints

NOTE: I use beet liquid instead of
boiling water for a better flavor
and color.

*Delmar Case, Fallbrook,
California (Del Mar Fair, Del
Mar, California)*

Harvard Beets

½ cup orange juice
1½ tablespoons cider vinegar
1 tablespoon honey
1 tablespoon cornstarch
½ teaspoon salt
½ teaspoon cloves
1 pint (2 cups) Canned Beets, drained
1 tablespoon butter or margarine

Combine all ingredients except beets and butter in the top of a double boiler; cook over boiling water, stirring until mixture is smooth. Adjust seasonings to your taste (mixture should be sweet-and-sour) and continue simmering and stirring until clear. Add beets; reduce heat and cook until beets are heated through. Just before serving, stir in butter or margarine.

Yield: 2 to 3 servings

Delmar Case, Fallbrook, California (Del Mar Fair, Del Mar, California)

Marinated Beet Salad

1 quart (4 cups) sliced Canned Beets
½ cup sugar
2½ teaspoons dry mustard
½ teaspoon salt
¾ cup vinegar
½ cup finely chopped onion
¼ cup finely chopped celery

Drain beets, reserving ½ cup liquid. Combine sugar, mustard, and salt in a saucepan; add reserved beet liquid and vinegar. Bring mixture to a boil, then remove from heat. Combine beets, onion, and celery. Pour vinegar mixture over vegetables and toss gently. Cover and refrigerate overnight.

Yield: 8 servings

Lillian Calhoun, Coushatta, Louisiana (Red River Parish Fair, Coushatta, Louisiana)

Sweet-and-Sour Beets

1 pint (2 cups) Canned Beets
1 tablespoon cornstarch
¼ teaspoon salt
2 tablespoons juice from beets
4 tablespoons honey
2 tablespoons vinegar
1 tablespoon butter or margarine

Drain beets, reserving 2 tablespoons juice. Combine cornstarch, salt, and beet juice in a saucepan. Stir in honey, vinegar, and butter or margarine; cook over low heat until mixture thickens. Pour sauce over beets and let stand 1 hour to enhance flavor. Heat before serving.

Yield: 4 to 6 servings

Cathy Grant, Wasilla, Alaska (Alaska State Fair, Palmer, Alaska)

Canned Carrots

11 pounds fresh carrots
Salt (optional)

Prepare home canning jars and lids according to manufacturer's instructions.

Wash and peel carrots. Pack whole carrots upright into hot jars, leaving one-inch headspace. Add ½ teaspoon salt to each pint, if desired. Cover with boiling water, leaving one-inch headspace. Remove air bubbles with a non-metallic spatula. Adjust caps.

Process pints 25 minutes at 10 pounds pressure in a pressure canner.

Yield: about 7 pints

Rebecca Hoffmann, Mesa, Arizona (Arizona State Fair, Phoenix, Arizona)

Carrot Casserole

1 quart (4 cups) Canned Carrots, drained
½ cup milk
6 tablespoons margarine, divided
4 cups bread crumbs

Preheat oven to 350°F.

Cut carrots into two-inch pieces and place in a saucepan; cover with hot tap water. Bring to a boil and boil hard for 10 minutes; drain thoroughly. With a mixer, mash carrots as if you were mashing potatoes. Add milk and 3 tablespoons margarine; whip together. Grease an 8 × 8-inch baking dish with 1 tablespoon margarine. Spread whipped carrot mixture in baking dish.

Place bread crumbs in a large plastic bag; using a rolling pin, crush bread until crumbs are quite small and fine. Sprinkle 2 cups of the fine crumbs over carrot mixture. Dot with remaining 2 tablespoons margarine.

Bake on top oven rack at 350°F until top is browned (20 to 35 minutes). Serve piping hot.

Yield: 6 to 8 servings

Madonna Joy Wilson, Fontana, California (Los Angeles County Fair, Pomona, California)

Carrot Ring

1 pint (2 cups) Canned Carrots, drained
  and diced
½ teaspoon minced onion
1 teaspoon salt
⅛ teaspoon pepper
3 eggs, well beaten
1 cup milk
Seasoned cooked peas

Preheat oven to 350°F.

Combine all ingredients except peas; mix well. Pour mixture into a buttered ring mold.

Bake at 350°F for 40 minutes. To serve, remove from mold, place on serving platter, and fill center with seasoned cooked peas.

Yield: 4 servings

NOTE: This is an attractive addition to a dinner table—especially at Thanksgiving or Christmastime.

*Irene Robison, Woodstock, Maryland
(Maryland State Fair, Timonium,
Maryland)*

Citrus Spiced Carrots

2 pints (4 cups) Canned Carrots
½ cup pineapple juice
½ cup orange juice
¼ cup honey
¼ teaspoon allspice
⅛ teaspoon nutmeg
2 tablespoons cornstarch
Bread crumbs

Preheat oven to 350°F.

Drain carrots; set aside. Combine pineapple juice, orange juice, honey, allspice, and nutmeg; stir in cornstarch. Place carrots in a greased two-quart casserole dish. Pour juice mixture over carrots.

Bake at 350°F for 20 minutes. Garnish with bread crumbs and continue baking until crumbs are golden brown.

Yield: 6 to 8 servings

Ball Recipe

Canned Summer Squash

21 pounds summer squash
(zucchini, crookneck or yellow
squash)
Salt (optional)

Prepare home canning jars and lids according to manufacturer's instructions.

Wash squash and cut into small pieces; do not peel. Steam or boil 2 or 3 minutes. Pack hot squash into hot jars, leaving one-inch headspace. Add 1 teaspoon salt to each quart (½ teaspoon salt to each pint), if desired. Cover with boiling water, leaving one-inch headspace. Remove air bubbles with a non-metallic spatula. Adjust caps.

Process quarts 40 minutes at 10 pounds pressure in a pressure canner.

Yield: about 7 quarts

Ball Recipe

Cream of Zucchini Soup

1 quart (4 cups) Canned Zucchini,
   drained
1 tablespoon grated onion
2 tablespoons butter or margarine
2 tablespoons all-purpose flour
4 cups milk
¾ teaspoon salt
¼ teaspoon white pepper
¼ teaspoon celery salt
⅛ teaspoon garlic powder
3 teaspoons grated Parmesan cheese
¾ teaspoon paprika

Place zucchini in a saucepan; cover with water. Bring to a boil and boil hard for 10 minutes; drain thoroughly. Press zucchini through a strainer, saving all of the pulp; set aside.

Sauté onion in butter or margarine for approximately 2 minutes. Blend in flour. Gradually add milk, stirring constantly. Measure 2 cups zucchini pulp; add to milk mixture along with salt, pepper, celery salt, and garlic powder. Cook, stirring constantly, until soup thickens. Ladle soup into soup bowls. Sprinkle with Parmesan cheese and paprika. Serve immediately.

Yield: 6 servings

*Madonna Joy Wilson, Fontana, California
(Los Angeles County Fair, Pomona,
California)*

Squash Delight Casserole

1 quart (4 cups) Canned Squash, drained
½ cup chopped sweet green pepper
½ cup chopped pimientos
½ cup chopped onion
½ cup chopped pecans
½ cup mayonnaise
1 egg
¼ cup (½ stick) butter or margarine
1 teaspoon sugar
½ teaspoon salt
Dash of pepper
½ cup bread crumbs
½ cup grated cheese

Preheat oven to 350°F.

Combine squash with all remaining ingredients except bread crumbs and cheese. Spoon mixture into a buttered 1½-quart baking dish. Sprinkle with bread crumbs and grated cheese.

Bake at 350°F for 30 minutes.

Yield: 6 servings

*Estelle W. Bragg, Vienna, Georgia
(Central Georgia Fair, Cordele, Georgia)*

Canned Yams

4 large, long, brown-skinned yams per quart

Prepare home canning jars and lids according to manufacturer's instructions.

Wash yams well and place in a large saucepan; cover with water and boil 20 to 25 minutes. Remove skins, trim off ends, and cut yams into uniform slices about one inch thick. Pack yam slices tightly into hot quart jars. Cover with boiling water, leaving one-inch headspace. Remove air bubbles with a non-metallic spatula. Adjust caps.

Process quarts 1 hour and 30 minutes at 10 pounds pressure in a pressure canner.

NOTE: Reserve trimmed-off ends of yams to serve mashed and topped with butter.

Madonna Joy Wilson, Fontana, California (Los Angeles County Fair, Pomona, California)

Candied Yams

1 quart Canned Yams
½ pound (1⅓ cups) brown sugar
3 tablespoons butter or margarine
1½ cups white miniature marshmallows

Preheat oven to 350°F.

Place yams and liquid in a saucepan and boil gently for 10 minutes; drain yams, reserving liquid. Arrange yams in a buttered flat baking dish. Sprinkle brown sugar over yams. Heat reserved liquid and pour over yams to make ½ inch of liquid in baking dish. Discard any remaining liquid. Dot yams with margarine.

Cover and bake on center rack of oven at 350°F until liquid in baking dish starts to boil (25 to 30 minutes). Sprinkle marshmallows over yams and continue to bake, uncovered, for a few minutes or until marshmallows start to melt and turn golden brown.

Yield: 5 to 6 servings

Madonna Joy Wilson, Fontana, California (Los Angeles County Fair, Pomona, California)

Canned Mixed Vegetables

6 cups chopped tomatoes (8 to 10
  large tomatoes)
3 cups sliced zucchini (3 small
  zucchini)
2 cups sliced celery (2 large stalks)
2 cups sliced okra (6 to 7 pods,
  each 3 to 4 inches in length)
1 cup chopped onion

Prepare home canning jars and
lids according to manufacturer's
instructions.

Prepare vegetables as follows:
Wash, core, and peel tomatoes.
Cut into quarters, then cut each
quarter into three pieces. Wash
and trim zucchini; do not peel.
Halve each squash lengthwise,
then cut into ½-inch slices. Wash
and trim celery. Cut stalks into ½-
inch slices. Wash and trim okra.
Cut each pod into ½-inch slices.
Trim, peel, and chop onion.

Combine all vegetables in a large
saucepan and bring to a boil. Boil
5 minutes, stirring occasionally.
Pour hot vegetables and liquid
into hot jars, leaving one-inch
headspace. (If short on liquid, add
boiling water to bring liquid to
correct level.) Remove air bubbles
with a non-metallic spatula.
Adjust caps.

Process 30 minutes at 10 pounds
pressure in a pressure canner.

Yield: about 6 pints

*Teresa Biggs, Boise, Idaho (Western
Idaho Fair, Boise, Idaho)*

Luanne's Chili

1 pound dry pinto beans
7 pounds tomatoes, peeled and
  chopped
2 large white onions, chopped
1 large sweet green pepper,
  chopped
1 teaspoon salt
1½ pounds ground beef, browned
  and drained
2 tablespoons chili powder (or to
  taste)

Prepare home canning jars and lids according to manufacturer's instructions.

Wash beans thoroughly. Combine beans and 9 cups water in a large saucepan; boil 2 minutes. Remove beans from heat and let soak 1 hour, then drain. Place tomatoes in a large stainless steel saucepan and bring to a boil. Add onion, green pepper, and salt; boil 5 minutes. Add beans, ground beef, and chili powder; simmer 30 minutes. Fill hot jars with hot chili, leaving one-inch headspace. Remove air bubbles with a non-metallic spatula. Adjust caps.

Process pints 1 hour and 15 minutes at 10 pounds pressure in a pressure canner.

Yield: about 14 pints

*Luanne Shafer, Otis, Colorado
(Eastern Colorado Round-Up,
Akron, Colorado)*

FRUITS

CANNED APPLES 36 ■ Apple Crisp 37 ■ Apple Praline Pie 37 ■ CANNED APPLESAUCE 38 ■ Applesauce Cake 39 ■ Applesauce Honey Bread 40 ■ CANNED APRICOTS 41 ■ Apricot Fritters 42 ■ Apricot Cake 42 ■ CANNED BLACKBERRIES 43 ■ Blackberry Cream Sherbet 44 ■ Light Blackberry Pie 45 ■ CANNED CHERRIES 46 ■ Cherry Fruit Pie 47 ■ CANNED WHOLE CRANBERRY SAUCE 48 ■ Spicy Cranberry Dip 48 ■ CANNED GRAPE JUICE 49 ■ CANNED HOLIDAY MINCEMEAT 50 ■ Holiday Mince Pie 50 ■ Mincemeat Nut Bread 51 ■ Holiday Mincemeat Squares 51 ■ CANNED PEACHES 52 ■ Busy Homemaker's Peach Cobbler 53 ■ Peach Cobbler 53 ■ Coconut-Pecan Peach Cobbler 54 ■ Fruit Salad 55 ■ CANNED PEARS 56 ■ Rosy Pear Compote 57 ■ CANNED PINEAPPLE PEARS 58 ■ Amaretto Pear Cake with Caramel Sauce 59 ■ CANNED CHUNKY PEAR SAUCE 60 ■ Country Cobbler 61 ■ CANNED SPIKED PEAR MINCEMEAT 62 ■ Pear Mincemeat Tart 63 ■ CANNED PINEAPPLE 64 ■ Banana Split Cake 65 ■ CANNED PLUMS 66 ■ Plum Upside-Down Cake 67 ■ CANNED RED RASPBERRIES 68 ■ Chocolate Raspberry Dream Cake 69

FRUITS

Canned Apples

21 pounds apples
Light syrup

Prepare home canning jars and lids according to manufacturer's instructions.

Wash, peel, core, and slice apples. Place apple slices in soaking solution to prevent darkening. To prepare syrup, combine sugar and water in a saucepan; simmer until sugar dissolves. Drain apples and add to syrup; boil 5 minutes. Pack hot apple slices into hot jars, leaving ½-inch headspace. Cover with boiling syrup, leaving ½-inch headspace. Remove air bubbles with a non-metallic spatula. Adjust caps.

Process pints or quarts 20 minutes in a boiling water bath canner.

Yield: about 14 pints (about 7 quarts)

Ball Recipe

Apple Crisp

1 quart (4 cups) Canned Apples
¼ cup water
1 teaspoon cinnamon
½ teaspoon salt
1 cup sugar
½ cup sifted flour
⅓ cup butter or margarine, softened

Preheat oven to 350°F.

Arrange apples in the bottom of an 8 × 8-inch pan. Mix water, cinnamon, and salt; sprinkle over apples. Combine sugar, flour, and butter or margarine in a mixing bowl; using a pastry blender, work together until crumbly. Spread crumb mixture over apples.

Bake uncovered at 350°F for 25 minutes or until top is browned.

Yield: 6 servings

Mrs. Floyd Mounts, Oklahoma City, Oklahoma (State Fair of Oklahoma, Oklahoma City, Oklahoma)

Apple Praline Pie

Pastry for 1 (9 inch) pie shell
1½ quarts (6 cups) Canned Apples
½ cup sugar
5 tablespoons flour
½ teaspoon cinnamon
½ teaspoon ginger
¼ teaspoon salt
1 tablespoon lemon juice
⅓ cup plus 2 tablespoons butter or
   margarine, divided
⅔ cup packed brown sugar
⅔ cup chopped pecans

Preheat oven to 400°F.

Line a pie plate with pastry; prick sides and bottom with a fork. Bake at 400°F for 5 minutes; set aside.

Combine apples, sugar, flour, cinnamon, ginger, salt, and lemon juice; mix well. Spoon apples into pastry shell; dot with 2 tablespoons butter or margarine.

Bake at 400°F for 45 minutes.

Melt ⅓ cup butter or margarine in a small saucepan; stir in brown sugar. Bring slowly to a boil, stirring constantly; add pecans. Pour topping over pie and continue baking 5 minutes longer or until topping bubbles.

Yield: 9 servings

Ball Recipe

Canned Applesauce

8 pounds apples
½ cup water
½ cup sugar (optional)

Prepare home canning jars and lids according to manufacturer's instructions.

Wash, peel, core, and quarter apples. Combine apples and water in a large pot; cover and simmer until apples are tender. Press apples through a sieve or food mill. Combine apple pulp and sugar in large pot; bring to a boil. Pour hot applesauce into hot jars, leaving ½-inch headspace. Remove air bubbles with a non-metallic spatula. Adjust caps.

Process pints or quarts 20 minutes in a boiling water bath canner.

Yield: about 7 pints (about 3 quarts)

Ball Recipe

Applesauce Cake

1 cup sugar
¼ cup brown sugar
½ cup shortening
2 eggs
1 pint (2 cups) Canned Applesauce
  (unsweetened)
2 cups flour
2 teaspoons baking soda
1 teaspoon cinnamon
½ teaspoon cloves
½ teaspoon salt
1 teaspoon vanilla
1 teaspoon lemon extract
½ cup chopped walnuts
½ cup raisins (optional)
Confectioners' sugar frosting (optional)

Preheat oven to 350°F. Grease and flour two nine-inch cake pans or one 9 × 13-inch cake pan; set aside.

Mix sugar, brown sugar, shortening, and eggs, creaming well. Add applesauce and mix well. Combine flour, baking soda, cinnamon, cloves, and salt; sift together. Add dry ingredients to creamed mixture; mix well. Add vanilla and lemon extract; mix well. Stir in walnuts and raisins; mix to combine thoroughly. Spread batter in prepared pan(s).

Bake at 350°F for 45 to 55 minutes. Do not overbake. Spread cooled cake with a thin layer of confectioners' sugar frosting, if desired.

NOTE: Golden Delicious and Jonathan apples are the best for applesauce and applesauce cake.

*Mamie Trefry, Wenatchee, Washington
(North Central Washington District Fair,
Waterville, Washington)*

Applesauce Honey Bread

½ cup (1 stick) butter or margarine
½ cup brown sugar
1 egg
½ cup honey
¾ cup buttermilk
2 teaspoons baking soda
2 cups all-purpose flour
1 teaspoon cinnamon
1 teaspoon allspice
½ pint (1 cup) Canned Applesauce
½ cup chopped walnuts

Preheat oven to 350°F. Grease bottom and sides of a 9x5x2¾-inch loaf pan; set aside.

Cream butter or margarine and brown sugar in a large bowl. Add egg and beat well. Stir in honey. Combine buttermilk and soda; set aside. Combine flour, cinnamon, and allspice; add to creamed mixture alternately with buttermilk, beginning and ending with flour. Stir in applesauce and walnuts. Pour batter into prepared pan.

Bake at 350°F for 50 to 60 minutes or until a wooden pick inserted in center comes out clean. Cool 10 minutes on a wire rack, then remove from pan and continue cooling on rack.

Yield: 1 loaf

Ball Recipe

Canned Apricots

18 pounds ripe apricots
Medium syrup

Prepare home canning jars and lids according to manufacturer's instructions.

Wash and scald apricots. Remove skins, then halve and pit apricots. Place apricot halves in soaking solution to prevent darkening. To prepare syrup, combine sugar and water in a saucepan; cook until sugar dissolves. Add a few apricot halves at a time to syrup; heat until thoroughly hot. Pack hot apricot halves into hot jars, leaving ½-inch headspace. Cover with boiling syrup, leaving ½-inch headspace. Remove air bubbles with a non-metallic spatula. Adjust caps.

Process quarts 25 minutes (pints 20 minutes) in a boiling water bath canner.

Yield: about 7 quarts (about 14 pints)

Terry Swann, Selbyville, Delaware (Delaware State Fair, Harrington, Delaware)

Apricot Fritters

1 quart (4 cups) Canned Apricots
1 egg
⅔ cup milk
1 tablespoon vegetable shortening, melted
1 cup flour
2 tablespoons sugar
1 teaspoon baking powder
¼ teaspoon salt
Vegetable shortening for deep-frying
Confectioners' sugar

Place vegetable shortening in deep-fryer and heat to 365°F.

Drain apricots on paper towels until they are as dry as possible. Beat egg with milk; stir in vegetable shortening. Combine flour, sugar, baking powder, and salt. Add dry ingredients to egg mixture, stirring just until mixed. Dip apricots in batter. Place a few batter-covered apricots at a time in hot shortening; turn once while cooking, frying until fritters are brown (about 4 minutes). Drain browned fritters on paper towels, then roll in confectioners' sugar. Serve warm.

Yield: 16 to 18 fritters

Terry Swann, Selbyville, Delaware (Delaware State Fair, Harrington, Delaware)

Apricot Cake

1 cup sugar
1 cup vegetable oil
2 eggs, beaten
2 cups flour
2 teaspoons baking soda
1 teaspoon cloves
1 teaspoon cinnamon
¼ teaspoon salt
1 pint (2 cups) Canned Apricots
1 cup chopped pecans
Whipped cream (optional)

Preheat oven to 375°F. Grease a 9 × 13-inch pan; set aside.

Mix sugar and oil; add eggs and mix well. Sift together flour, baking soda, cloves, cinnamon, and salt. Place undrained apricots in blender container and purée. Add dry ingredients alternately with apricot purée to creamed mixture; mix well. Stir in pecans. Spread batter in greased pan.

Bake at 375°F for 20 minutes. Serve cake with whipped cream, if desired.

NOTE: Use apricots canned in medium or heavy syrup.

Elizabeth Miles, Mesa, Arizona (Arizona State Fair, Phoenix, Arizona)

Canned Blackberries

2 quarts firm, ripe blackberries
Light syrup
2 teaspoons lemon juice

Prepare home canning jars and lids according to manufacturer's instructions.

Wash blackberries in cold water; drain. To prepare syrup, combine sugar and water in a medium saucepan; cook over medium heat until sugar dissolves (about 5 minutes). Reduce heat to low.

Pack blackberries into hot jars, leaving ½-inch headspace. Shake jars gently to settle fruit. Add ½ teaspoon lemon juice to each jar. Pour hot syrup over berries, leaving ½-inch headspace. Remove air bubbles with a non-metallic spatula. Adjust caps.

Process pints 15 minutes in a boiling water bath canner.

Yield: about 4 pints

NOTE: Work with less than a gallon of fruit at a time. Having jars clean and hot before starting is a must.

Gail Marie Holmes-Lee, Bardstown, Kentucky (Nelson County Fair, Bardstown, Kentucky)

Blackberry Cream Sherbet

SHERBET

1½ cups milk, at room temperature
1 cup sugar
1 pint (2 cups) Canned Blackberries, drained (reserve juice)
3 tablespoons lemon juice or Key lime juice
3 egg whites, at room temperature
1 cup cream, whipped

TOPPING

¾ cup reserved blackberry juice (add water to juice, if necessary, to make ¾ cup)
2 tablespoons cornstarch
3 tablespoons sugar
1 teaspoon lemon juice
¼ cup chopped walnuts

To make Sherbet: Combine milk and sugar in a saucepan; heat until sugar dissolves (about 3 minutes). Cool milk for 10 minutes, then pour into freezer trays or a small cake pan and partially freeze (about 90 minutes). Press blackberries through a sieve; set purée aside and discard seeds. Spoon frozen milk mixture into a cold bowl and beat with a wire whisk until mixture is light, adding blackberry purée and lemon juice as you beat. Pour mixture into same freezer trays or small cake pan and partially freeze again (about 45 minutes).

Using a mixer, beat egg whites until they are firm but not dry. Add whipped cream to egg whites and mix gently to combine. Spoon partially frozen blackberry mixture into a cold bowl; beat with a wire whisk just until softened. Fold egg white and whipped cream mixture into blackberry mixture. Spoon sherbet into a two-quart freezer container and freeze overnight or until firm.

To make Topping: In a saucepan, combine blackberry juice, cornstarch, sugar, lemon juice, and walnuts. Cook over medium heat until mixture thickens. Cool. Spoon over sherbet just before serving.

Yield: 8 to 12 servings

NOTE: Place a stainless steel bowl in a larger bowl filled with ice to keep frozen mixture cold while beating.

Gail Marie Holmes-Lee, Bardstown, Kentucky (Nelson County Fair, Bardstown, Kentucky)

Light Blackberry Pie

1 (3 ounce) package blackberry flavored
  gelatin
⅔ cup boiling water
2 cups crushed ice cubes
3½ cups whipped topping
½ pint (1 cup) Canned Blackberries,
  drained
1 graham cracker pie crust
Blackberries for garnish (optional)

Combine gelatin and boiling water; stir until gelatin dissolves (about 3 minutes). Add ice cubes and stir continuously for 2 to 3 minutes or until gelatin thickens; remove any unmelted ice. Using a wire whisk, blend in whipped topping; whip until smooth. Fold blackberries into mixture; refrigerate until chilled. Spoon filling into pie crust; chill 2 hours. Garnish with blackberries before serving, if desired.

Yield: 6 to 8 servings

NOTE: You can use canned, frozen, or fresh blackberries. If blackberry flavored gelatin is not available, black cherry is a good substitute.

Anne E. Cooper, Hayden, Idaho (North Idaho Fair, Coeur d'Alene, Idaho)

Canned Cherries

3 pounds pie cherries
Medium syrup

Prepare home canning jars and lids according to manufacturer's instructions.

Clean and pit cherries. To prepare syrup, combine sugar and water in a saucepan; simmer until sugar dissolves. Pour about ½ cup boiling syrup into hot jars. Pack cherries into jars, leaving ½-inch headspace. Shake jars to pack cherries closely without crushing. Add more boiling syrup, if needed, leaving ½-inch headspace. Remove air bubbles with a non-metallic spatula. Adjust caps.

Process pints 20 minutes in a boiling water bath canner.

Yield: about 5 pints

Connie Morgan, Horseshoe Bend, Idaho (Western Idaho Fair, Boise, Idaho)

Cherry Fruit Pie

CRUST

½ cup butter or margarine, melted
3 cups finely crushed graham cracker
  crumbs

FILLING

1 pint (2 cups) Canned Cherries, drained
1 (20 ounce) can crushed pineapple (do
  not drain)
1¼ cups sugar
2 tablespoons flour
1 small package orange flavored gelatin
6 bananas, thinly sliced
½ cup chopped walnuts
Whipped topping (optional)

Preheat oven to 375°F.

To make Crust: Combine butter or
margarine and crumbs; mix well. Pat
crumb mixture evenly into two nine-inch
pie pans. Bake at 375°F for 8 minutes.
Cool.

To make Filling: Combine cherries,
pineapple, sugar, and flour in a saucepan;
simmer over medium heat until mixture
thickens (about 20 minutes). Stir in dry
gelatin. Refrigerate mixture just until it
starts to jell. Add sliced bananas and
walnuts; mix well. Pour filling into pie
crusts; refrigerate until firm.

NOTE: Make crusts first so they can cool
while you are making the filling. Top pie
with whipped topping before serving, if
desired.

Connie Morgan, Horseshoe Bend, Idaho
(Western Idaho Fair, Boise, Idaho)

Canned Whole Cranberry Sauce

8 cups cranberries
4 cups sugar
4 cups water

Prepare home canning jars and lids according to manufacturer's instructions.

Wash, sort, and stem berries. Combine sugar and water in a large pot; boil 5 minutes. Add berries to syrup and boil, without stirring, until skins burst. Pour hot cranberry sauce into hot jars, leaving 1/4-inch headspace. Adjust caps.

Process pints 10 minutes in a boiling water bath canner.

Yield: about 6 pints

Ball Recipe

Spicy Cranberry Dip

1 pint (2 cups) Canned Whole Cranberry Sauce
1/4 pint (1/2 cup) Canned Chili Sauce (Ball Recipe)
1 tablespoon fresh lemon juice
2 teaspoons prepared horseradish
2 teaspoons Dijon mustard

Combine all ingredients in a saucepan; heat to boiling, stirring constantly. Serve hot as a dip.

Yield: 2 cups

NOTE: This spicy dip is great with fried breaded shrimp.

Ball Recipe

Canned Grape Juice

10 pounds ripe Concord grapes
2 quarts cold water
4 cups sugar

Prepare home canning jars and lids according to manufacturer's instructions.

Wash and stem grapes. Combine grapes and water in a large kettle and bring to a boil. Boil slowly for 15 minutes. Pour grapes and water into a loosely woven juice bag and squeeze out juice well. Return juice to kettle; add sugar and bring to a boil. Boil 10 minutes. Pour hot juice into hot jars, leaving ¼-inch headspace. Adjust caps.

Process quarts 15 minutes in a boiling water bath canner.

Yield: about 5 quarts

NOTE: To serve, dilute juice with an equal amount of water. Serve cold.

*Gladys Reisinger, Waterloo, Iowa
(National Cattle Congress
Exposition, Waterloo, Iowa)*

Canned Holiday Mincemeat

4 pounds apples, peeled, cored
  and chopped
4 pounds pears, peeled, cored and
  chopped
2 (15 ounce) packages raisins
2 cups brown sugar
Juice and grated peel of 2 oranges
Juice and grated peel of 2 lemons
4 teaspoons cinnamon
2 teaspoons cloves
1 teaspoon allspice
1 teaspoon nutmeg
1 teaspoon ginger

Combine all ingredients in a large saucepot; simmer 1 hour, stirring frequently to prevent sticking.

Prepare home canning jars and lids according to manufacturer's instructions.

Pour hot mincemeat into hot jars, leaving ¼-inch headspace. Remove air bubbles with a non-metallic spatula. Adjust caps.

Process pints 25 minutes in a boiling water bath canner.

Yield: about 8 pints

Ball Recipe

Holiday Mince Pie

Pastry for 1 (9 inch) double-crust pie
2 pints (4 cups) Canned Holiday
  Mincemeat

Preheat oven to 425°F.

Prepare pastry using your favorite recipe. Line a pie plate with half of the pastry. Pour mincemeat evenly over bottom crust. Cover with top crust; seal and flute edges.

Bake at 425°F about 35 minutes.

Yield: 9 servings

Ball Recipe

Mincemeat Nut Bread

1½ cups all-purpose flour
¾ cup sugar
2½ teaspoons baking powder
½ teaspoon salt
½ teaspoon cinnamon
2 eggs, lightly beaten
3 tablespoons shortening, melted and cooled
1 teaspoon vanilla
¾ pint (1½ cups) Canned Holiday Mincemeat
½ cup chopped walnuts

Preheat oven to 350°F. Grease a 9x5-inch loaf pan; set aside.

Combine flour, sugar, baking powder, salt, and cinnamon; sift together into a large bowl. Combine eggs, shortening, and vanilla in a medium bowl; stir in mincemeat and nuts. Combine mincemeat mixture with dry ingredients, stirring only enough to moisten flour. Pour batter into prepared pan.

Bake at 350°F for 60 to 70 minutes. Set pan on a wire rack to cool 10 minutes, then remove bread from pan and cool completely.

Yield: 1 loaf

Ball Recipe

Holiday Mincemeat Squares

1½ cups uncooked rolled oats (quick-cooking or old-fashioned)
1 cup all-purpose flour
½ cup (1 stick) butter or margarine, softened
¼ cup light brown sugar
¼ cup milk
½ teaspoon grated lemon peel
½ teaspoon coriander
½ teaspoon cinnamon
½ teaspoon nutmeg
¼ teaspoon salt
¼ teaspoon baking soda
1 pint (2 cups) Canned Holiday Mincemeat

Preheat oven to 350°F. Grease an 8x8-inch pan; set aside.

Combine all ingredients except mincemeat in a large bowl; mix at medium speed of electric mixer until well blended. Place half of the oat mixture in greased pan and gently pat into an even layer. Spoon mincemeat evenly over oat layer. Top with remaining oat mixture and gently pat into an even layer.

Bake at 350°F for 25 to 30 minutes. Set pan on a wire rack to cool. Cut into squares to serve.

Yield: 16 squares

Ball Recipe

Canned Peaches

24 pounds firm, ripe peaches
Lemon juice
Medium syrup

Prepare home canning jars and lids according to manufacturer's instructions.

Wash peaches. Place peaches in cold water mixed with 2 tablespoons lemon juice and let stand 20 minutes. After lemon bath, place peaches in boiling water for 1½ to 2 minutes to loosen skins. Dip peaches in cold water, then remove skins, cut out pits, and scrape cavities. Place peach halves in cold water mixed with 2 tablespoons lemon juice.

To prepare syrup, combine sugar and water in a saucepan; bring to a boil. Using a wooden spoon, pack peach halves, cavity side down, into hot jars in overlapping layers, leaving ½-inch headspace. Cover peaches with boiling syrup, leaving ½-inch headspace. Remove air bubbles with a non-metallic spatula. Adjust caps.

Process quarts 30 minutes in a boiling water bath canner.

Yield: about 12 quarts

NOTE: Letting peaches stand in water mixed with lemon juice after washing and again after the skins are removed preserves their beautiful, fresh color.

Kaye Heeb, Harrisburg, Arkansas (Northeast Arkansas District Fair, Jonesboro, Arkansas)

Busy Homemaker's Peach Cobbler

1 cup flour
1 cup sugar
½ teaspoon cinnamon
½ teaspoon apple pie spice
1 cup milk
1 teaspoon vanilla
½ cup (1 stick) margarine
1 quart (4 cups) Canned Peaches

Preheat oven to 350°F.

Combine flour, sugar, cinnamon, and apple pie spice; add milk and stir until batter is smooth and lump free. Stir in vanilla. Melt margarine in a two-quart baking dish. Arrange peaches in butter in baking dish. Pour batter over peaches.

Bake at 350°F for 35 to 45 minutes or until browned. Serve hot, plain or with ice cream.

Yield: 8 servings

NOTE: For a more elegant dessert, reduce amount of milk to ½ cup and add ½ cup apricot brandy.

Kaye Heeb, Harrisburg, Arkansas (Northeast Arkansas District Fair, Jonesboro, Arkansas)

Peach Cobbler

½ cup (1 stick) butter or margarine
1 cup sugar
1 cup flour
1½ teaspoons baking powder
¼ teaspoon salt
¾ cup milk
1 quart (4 cups) sliced Canned Peaches

Preheat oven to 350°F.

Melt butter or margarine in a 9 × 13-inch baking dish or pan. Combine sugar, flour, baking powder, salt, and milk in a mixing bowl; mix well. Pour batter into baking dish. Arrange peaches on top of batter.

Bake at 350°F for 30 to 40 minutes.

Yield: 8 servings

Nancy Johnson, Clever, Missouri (Missouri State Fair, Sedalia, Missouri)

Coconut-Pecan Peach Cobbler

2 tablespoons butter or margarine, melted
1 cup all-purpose flour
1 cup sugar
3 teaspoons baking powder
¼ teaspoon salt
¾ cup milk
1 pint (2 cups) sliced Canned Peaches
¼ cup pecans
⅓ cup coconut

Preheat oven to 350°F. Grease a large baking dish with butter or margarine; set aside.

Combine flour, sugar, baking powder, and salt; sift together into a mixing bowl. Add milk to dry ingredients and stir until batter is smooth. Pour batter into greased baking dish. Spoon peaches and juice over batter.

Bake at 350°F for 30 minutes. Sprinkle pecans and coconut over cobbler and continue baking 10 minutes longer.

Yield: 6 to 8 servings

Eugenia Whitlow, Knob Lick, Kentucky (Metcalfe County Fair, Edmonton, Kentucky)

Fruit Salad

(Microwave Recipe)

1 pint (2 cups) sliced Canned Peaches
1 (20 ounce) can pineapple chunks
2 (11 ounce) cans mandarin oranges
1 (3⅛ ounce) package vanilla pudding
  (not instant pudding)
1 (3 ounce) package strawberry flavored
  gelatin
1½ tablespoons minute tapioca
1 small package frozen strawberries,
  thawed
2 bananas, sliced

Drain peaches, pineapple, and oranges, reserving juices; set fruit aside. Measure 2 cups of the juices and pour into a two-quart glass baking dish. Add pudding mix, gelatin, and tapioca; stir to combine. Let mixture stand 5 minutes, then stir again. Microwave on High until mixture thickens, stirring often. Cool. Add drained fruit, strawberries, and bananas; mix well. Refrigerate.

Yield: 12 servings

NOTE: Pudding mixture can also be cooked in a saucepan on the stove. This salad can be refrigerated for up to a week in a covered container.

Vyla Blough, Waterloo, Iowa (National Cattle Congress Exposition, Waterloo, Iowa)

Canned Pears

2 tablespoons vinegar
2 tablespoons salt
4 quarts cold water
6 pounds Bartlett pears
Heavy syrup

Prepare home canning jars and lids according to manufacturer's instructions.

Combine vinegar, salt, and water. Wash, peel, halve, and core pears. Dip pear halves in vinegar solution to prevent darkening.

To prepare syrup, combine sugar and water in a saucepan; heat to a boil, stirring constantly until sugar dissolves. Pack pear halves, cut side down, into hot jars, leaving ½-inch headspace. Cover with hot syrup, leaving ½-inch headspace. Remove air bubbles with a non-metallic spatula. Adjust caps.

Process quarts 25 minutes in a boiling water bath canner.

Yield: about 3 quarts

Warren L. Knudtson, Las Vegas, Nevada (Las Vegas Jaycees State Fair, Las Vegas, Nevada)

Rosy Pear Compote

2 medium oranges
1 quart (4 cups) Canned Pears
1 pint (2 cups) Canned Whole Cranberry
 Sauce
⅓ cup sugar
1 tablespoon lemon juice
¼ teaspoon cinnamon
¼ teaspoon ginger

Preheat oven to 350°F.

Peel oranges and separate into sections; cut sections in half. Combine oranges and pears in a 1½-quart baking dish. In a medium saucepan, combine cranberry sauce, sugar, lemon juice, cinnamon, and ginger; bring to a boil. Pour hot cranberry mixture over fruit in baking dish.

Cover dish and bake at 350°F for 30 minutes. Serve warm.

Yield: 6 servings

*Warren L. Knudtson, Las Vegas, Nevada
(Las Vegas Jaycees State Fair, Las Vegas, Nevada)*

Canned Pineapple Pears

3 tablespoons fruit preserver
2 quarts water
4 pounds firm, blemish-free
  Bartlett pears
2 quarts pineapple juice
½ cup sugar

Prepare home canning jars and lids according to manufacturer's instructions.

Mix fruit preserver with water. Wash, peel, halve, and core pears. Place pear halves in fruit preserver solution. (Leave pears in solution no longer than 20 minutes.)

To make syrup, combine pineapple juice and sugar in a large saucepan; boil until sugar dissolves. Add pear halves to syrup and cook 5 minutes. Pack hot pears, cut side down, into hot jars, leaving ½-inch headspace. Cover with boiling syrup, leaving ½-inch headspace. Remove air bubbles with a non-metallic spatula. Adjust caps.

Process pints 20 minutes in a boiling water bath canner.

Yield: about 6 pints

NOTE: The pineapple juice adds a nice flavor and a bit of tartness to the pears.

Nicol Alexander, Jonesborough, Tennessee (Appalachian Fair Association, Gray, Tennessee)

Amaretto Pear Cake with Caramel Sauce

CAKE

1 pint (2 cups) Canned Pineapple Pears or
    Canned Pears in light syrup
⅓ cup pear syrup (from canned pears)
1 package white cake mix with pudding
3 egg whites
⅓ cup vegetable oil
2 tablespoons almond liqueur

FROSTING

1 cup whipping cream
2 tablespoons sugar
2 tablespoons almond liqueur
1 pint (2 cups) Canned Pears, drained
½ cup chopped walnuts

SAUCE

½ cup (1 stick) butter or margarine
1 cup packed brown sugar
1 cup whipping cream
1 tablespoon almond liqueur

Preheat oven to 350°F. Grease and flour a ten-inch tube pan; set aside.

To make Cake: Drain pears, reserving ⅓ cup pear syrup; set syrup aside. Purée pears in food processor. In a large bowl, combine pear purée, reserved pear syrup, cake mix, egg whites, oil, and almond liqueur; mix 2 minutes at low speed of mixer. Pour batter into prepared tube pan.

Bake at 350°F for 40 minutes or until toothpick inserted in center comes out clean. Cool cake upright in pan for 15 minutes, then invert onto serving platter and cool completely.

To make Frosting: In a small bowl, beat whipping cream with sugar and almond liqueur until firm. Spread frosting over cooled cake. Cut pears into 32 slices. Arrange pear slices on top of cake, slightly overlapping the slices. Press chopped walnuts into frosting on sides of cake. Refrigerate until serving time.

To make Sauce: In a small saucepan, combine butter or margarine, brown sugar, and whipping cream. Heat to boiling and boil 5 minutes, stirring occasionally. Remove from heat and stir in almond liqueur; set aside until sauce cools slightly. Drizzle 4 tablespoons of sauce over pears on top of cake. Drizzle remaining sauce over individual slices of cake before serving.

Yield: 16 servings

NOTE: This cake has an unusual and delicate flavor. Store cake in refrigerator.

*Nicol Alexander, Jonesborough, Tennessee
(Appalachian Fair Association, Gray,
Tennessee)*

Canned Chunky Pear Sauce

6 pounds pears (Bartlett,
   D'Anjou or Bosc)
2 cups water
1 tablespoon bottled lemon juice
½ cup sugar (more or less to taste)

Prepare home canning jars and lids according to manufacturer's instructions.

Wash, peel, quarter, and core pears, then cut into slices. Combine water and lemon juice in a saucepan; add pears and cook over medium heat until tender (about 15 minutes), stirring to prevent sticking. Remove from heat and mash pears with a potato masher. Reheat over low heat. Add sugar to taste. Bring mixture to a boil over medium heat, stirring to prevent sticking. Spoon hot mixture into hot jars, leaving ½-inch headspace. Remove air bubbles with a non-metallic spatula. Adjust caps.

Process pints 20 minutes in a boiling water bath canner.

Yield: about 6 pints

NOTE: This is a nice change from applesauce, and it has the beautiful pear color.

Susan C. Moser, King, North Carolina (Dixie Classic Fair, Winston-Salem, North Carolina)

Country Cobbler

¾ stick (6 tablespoons) butter or
   margarine
1 cup sugar
1 cup self-rising flour
1 cup milk
1 pint (2 cups) Canned Chunky Pear
   Sauce
½ teaspoon cinnamon
Whipped topping or ice cream (optional)

Preheat oven to 350°F.

Melt butter or margarine in a 13 × 9-inch baking pan. Mix sugar, flour, and milk; stir until smooth. Pour batter over melted butter in baking pan; swirl to mix. Spoon pear sauce by tablespoonfuls over batter; swirl to mix pear sauce with batter. Sprinkle with cinnamon.

Bake at 350°F for 35 minutes or until lightly browned. Serve with whipped topping or ice cream, if desired.

Yield: 8 to 10 servings

NOTE: In place of the pear sauce, you can use 1 quart of drained peaches, pears, blackberries, cherries, apples, or blueberries.

Susan C. Moser, King, North Carolina (Dixie Classic Fair, Winston-Salem, North Carolina)

Canned Spiked Pear Mincemeat

7 pounds pears, peeled and cored
6 cups sugar
2½ cups golden raisins
2 cups chopped dates
2 cups chopped walnuts
1 orange, seeded and ground
1 tablespoon cinnamon
1 tablespoon nutmeg
2 teaspoons mace
1½ teaspoons ginger
1 cup brandy

Prepare home canning jars and lids according to manufacturer's instructions.

Coarsely chop pears. Combine pears with all ingredients except brandy in a large saucepot. Bring to a boil over medium-high heat, then reduce heat and simmer 90 minutes or until mixture is thick. Remove from heat; stir in brandy. Pour hot mincemeat into hot jars, leaving ¼-inch headspace. Remove air bubbles with a non-metallic spatula. Adjust caps.

Process quarts 30 minutes in a boiling water bath canner.

Yield: about 3 quarts

Ball Recipe

Pear Mincemeat Tart

1 cup (2 sticks) unsalted butter, softened
¾ cup superfine sugar
1 teaspoon vanilla
1½ cups all-purpose flour
½ cup cornstarch
¼ teaspoon salt
1 teaspoon grated lemon peel
1 teaspoon coriander
1½ pints (3 cups) Canned Spiked Pear
   Mincemeat

Preheat oven to 325°F.

Cream butter with sugar until fluffy; beat in vanilla. Combine flour, cornstarch, salt, lemon peel, and coriander; sift together. Add dry ingredients to creamed mixture and beat until well blended, being careful not to overwork the dough. Pat dough into a ten-inch tart pan; prick bottom and sides of crust with a fork.

Bake at 325°F for 40 to 45 minutes or until pale golden brown. Cool tart shell in pan 20 minutes, then remove shell from pan and cool completely. Fill cooled tart shell with mincemeat.

Yield: 10 servings

Ball Recipe

Canned Pineapple

3 quarts pineapple chunks, cut
  into ½-inch wedges
Light syrup
1 tablespoon fruit preserver

Prepare home canning jars and lids according to manufacturer's instructions.

Prepare pineapple; set aside. To make syrup, combine sugar and water in a small saucepan; boil 5 minutes. Add fruit preserver to syrup (this will keep pineapple from darkening). Combine pineapple and syrup in a large saucepan; simmer until pineapple is tender. Pack hot pineapple and syrup into hot jars, leaving ½-inch headspace. Remove air bubbles with a non-metallic spatula. Adjust caps.

Process pints 15 minutes in a boiling water bath canner.

Yield: about 5 pints

John L. Good, Richmond, Kansas (Kansas State Fair, Hutchinson, Kansas)

Banana Split Cake

CRUST

1 cup crushed vanilla wafer crumbs
¼ cup confectioners' sugar
¼ cup chopped black walnuts
¼ cup (½ stick) butter or margarine,
  melted

FILLING

2 eggs
1 cup confectioners' sugar
¼ cup (½ stick) butter or margarine,
  softened
2½ bananas
⅔ of ½-pint (⅔ cup) Canned Pineapple,
  drained and chopped

TOPPING

1 large carton whipped topping
½ teaspoon vanilla
¼ cup chopped walnuts
¼ cup chopped maraschino cherries

To make Crust: Combine vanilla wafer crumbs, confectioners' sugar, walnuts, and butter or margarine; mix well. Press mixture firmly into a buttered 9 × 9-inch baking dish.

To make Filling: Combine eggs, confectioners' sugar, and butter or margarine; beat at highest speed of electric mixer until thoroughly mixed. Pour filling over crust in baking dish. Cut bananas into slices lengthwise and arrange over filling. Spread pineapple evenly over bananas.

To make Topping: Stir vanilla into whipped topping; spread evenly over pineapple. Sprinkle walnuts and maraschino cherries over whipped topping. Refrigerate before serving.

Yield: 6 servings

John L. Good, Richmond, Kansas (Kansas State Fair, Hutchinson, Kansas)

Canned Plums

6 quarts plums
Heavy syrup

Prepare home canning jars and lids according to manufacturer's instructions.

Wash plums; prick with a clean needle to prevent fruit from bursting. To prepare syrup, combine sugar and water in a saucepan; cook over medium heat until sugar dissolves. Add plums and slowly bring to a boil. Cook plums in syrup at a low boil for 5 minutes. Using a slotted spoon, remove plums from syrup. Pack plums into hot jars, filling jars three-fourths full. Cover with boiling syrup, leaving ½-inch headspace. Remove air bubbles with a non-metallic spatula. Adjust caps.

Process pints 20 minutes in a boiling water bath canner.

Yield: 7 pints

NOTE: Fruit remains reasonably firm. You can use plum syrup as a topping for ice cream, or process it into jelly.

Julie Ann Ward, Washington Court House, Ohio (Ohio State Fair, Columbus, Ohio)

Plum Upside-Down Cake

1 pint (2 cups) Canned Plums
2 tablespoons butter or margarine
1¼ cups sugar
3 egg yolks
1¾ cups flour
2 teaspoons baking powder
⅓ cup plum syrup (from canned plums)
⅔ cup milk

Preheat oven to 350°F. Grease and flour an 8 × 8-inch baking pan; set aside.

Drain plums, reserving ⅓ cup syrup. Cut plums in half and discard pits. Cream butter or margarine with sugar until light; beat in egg yolks, one at a time. Combine flour and baking powder; sift together. Combine plum syrup and milk. Add milk mixture alternately with dry ingredients to creamed mixture; mix well. Layer plums, cut side up, in a decorative pattern in prepared pan. Slowly pour batter over plums.

Bake at 350°F for 25 to 30 minutes or until a toothpick inserted in center comes out clean. Place pan on a rack to cool for 5 minutes, then remove cake from pan and continue cooling.

Yield: 9 servings

NOTE: This cake can be served plain, but it is delicious served warm with whipped cream.

Julie Ann Ward, Washington Court House, Ohio (Ohio State Fair, Columbus, Ohio)

Canned Red Raspberries

6 pints red raspberries
Medium syrup

Prepare home canning jars and lids according to manufacturer's instructions.

Wash berries in ice-cold water, being careful to retain berries' shape; drain. While berries are draining, prepare syrup.

To prepare syrup, combine sugar and water in a saucepan; heat until sugar dissolves. Working quickly and carefully, pour about ½ cup hot syrup into each hot jar. Add berries to jars, then shake jars gently to pack tightly, being careful not to crush berries. Continue to add berries and shake jars, leaving ½-inch headspace. Add more syrup if needed, leaving ½-inch headspace. Remove air bubbles with a non-metallic spatula. Adjust caps.

Process pints 15 minutes in a boiling water bath canner.

Yield: about 6 pints

NOTE: These berries retain their color well—for up to twelve months. Fruit seldom floats.

Elizabeth A. Lynch, Boulder, Colorado (Colorado State Fair, Pueblo, Colorado)

Chocolate Raspberry Dream Cake

CAKE

1 package devil's food cake mix
1 package dark chocolate instant pudding
   mix
1¼ cups water
4 eggs
½ cup vegetable oil

FILLING

1½ pints (3 cups) Canned Red
   Raspberries
½ cup raspberry juice (from canned
   raspberries)
6 tablespoons cornstarch
1 cup sugar

FROSTING

3 cups sifted confectioners' sugar, divided
½ cup cocoa powder
½ cup (1 stick) butter or margarine,
   softened
¼ cup plus 2 tablespoons raspberry juice
   (from canned raspberries), divided

Preheat oven to 350°F. Grease and flour
two eight-inch round cake pans; set aside.

To make Cake: In a large mixing bowl,
combine cake mix, pudding mix, water,
eggs, and oil. Beat at medium speed of
electric mixer 2 minutes. Pour batter into
prepared pans.

Bake at 350°F for 45 minutes. Cool
completely.

To make Filling (while cake bakes and
cools): Drain raspberries, reserving juice. In
a small bowl, mix ½ cup raspberry juice
with cornstarch. (Set remaining juice aside
for frosting.) Combine raspberries and sugar
in a saucepan; bring to a boil. Stir in
cornstarch mixture and cook over medium
heat until very thick (about 5 minutes).
Chill. When cake is completely cool,
spread chilled filling between layers.

To make Frosting: In a mixing bowl,
combine 1 cup confectioners' sugar, cocoa
powder, butter or margarine, and 2
tablespoons raspberry juice; beat until
creamy. Gradually add remaining
confectioners' sugar and raspberry juice;
continue beating until smooth. Spread
frosting over top and sides of cake.

Yield: 20 servings

NOTE: You can substitute raspberry
liqueur for some of the raspberry juice in
the filling and frosting. Refrigerate any
leftover cake.

Elizabeth A. Lynch, Boulder, Colorado
(Colorado State Fair, Pueblo, Colorado)

TOMATOES

TOMATOES

Canned Tomatoes

21 pounds fresh, firm, red-ripe
   tomatoes
Bottled lemon juice or citric acid
Salt (optional)

Prepare home canning jars and lids according to manufacturer's instructions.

Raw Pack

Wash tomatoes. Dip tomatoes in boiling water for 30 to 60 seconds or until skins split, then dip in cold water. Slip off skins and remove cores. Leave tomatoes whole or cut into halves. Add 2 tablespoons bottled lemon juice or ½ teaspoon citric acid to each quart. (Add 1 tablespoon bottled lemon juice or ¼ teaspoon citric acid to each pint.) Pack tomatoes into hot jars and cover with hot water, leaving ½-inch headspace. Add 1 teaspoon salt to each quart (½ teaspoon salt to each pint), if desired. Remove air bubbles with a non-metallic spatula. Adjust caps.

Process quarts 45 minutes (pints 40 minutes) in a boiling water bath canner.

(continued)

Canned Tomatoes

(continued)

Hot Pack

Wash tomatoes. Dip tomatoes in boiling water for 30 to 60 seconds or until skins split, then dip in cold water. Slip off skins and remove cores. Leave tomatoes whole or cut into halves. Place tomatoes in a large saucepan; add enough water to cover. Boil gently 5 minutes, stirring to prevent sticking. Add 2 tablespoons bottled lemon juice or ½ teaspoon citric acid to each quart. (Add 1 tablespoon bottled lemon juice or ¼ teaspoon citric acid to each pint.) Pack hot tomatoes into hot jars, leaving ½-inch headspace. Cover with hot cooking liquid, leaving ½-inch headspace. Add 1 teaspoon salt to each quart (½ teaspoon salt to each pint), if desired. Remove air bubbles with a non-metallic spatula. Adjust caps.

Process quarts 45 minutes (pints 40 minutes) in a boiling water bath canner.

Yield: about 7 quarts (about 14 pints)

Ball Recipe prepared by Martha Bell, Pryor, Oklahoma (Tulsa State Fair, Tulsa, Oklahoma)

Preserver's Potluck

1 medium onion, chopped
1 clove garlic, minced
1 tablespoon vegetable oil
⅛ teaspoon freshly ground black pepper
1 quart (4 cups) Canned Tomatoes
2 cups frozen zucchini slices
2 cups frozen eggplant cubes
2 cups frozen sweet green pepper, cut into
   1-inch pieces
2 cups frozen okra slices
1 tablespoon dried parsley
1 pint (2 cups) Canned Green Beans,
   drained
Hot cooked noodles

Sauté onion and garlic in oil until translucent (about 5 minutes); add black pepper. Add tomatoes, zucchini, eggplant, green pepper, okra, and parsley; bring to a boil and simmer about 10 minutes. Add green beans and simmer 5 minutes longer. Serve over hot cooked noodles.

Yield: 6 servings

NOTE: No need to add salt if salt was used in canning. Cubes of any leftover meat or seafood make a hearty addition to this dish, but it is delicious and nutritious as is.

*Virginia A. Price, Jamesville, New York
(New York State Fair, Syracuse, New York)*

Chili Fringo

1½ pounds ground chuck
1 large onion, chopped
1 clove garlic, minced
1 sweet green pepper, chopped or sliced
1¼ teaspoons salt
1 teaspoon celery seed
½ teaspoon black pepper
1 quart (4 cups) Canned Tomatoes
2 (16 ounce) cans kidney beans, drained
2 (4 ounce) cans mushrooms, drained
   (optional)
½ cup (1 stick) butter or margarine

Brown chuck with onion and garlic; drain off all grease. Combine browned chuck with all remaining ingredients in a large stewing pan. Simmer on low heat for 4 hours, stirring occasionally. Serve with relishes and garlic bread.

NOTE: This chili can also be cooked all day in a slow cooker on low heat.

Arleen B. Owen, Fresno, California (The Big Fresno Fair, Fresno, California)

Tamale Pie

1 cup yellow cornmeal
3 cups cold water, divided
1 teaspoon salt, divided
1 tablespoon vegetable oil
½ pound lean ground beef
⅓ cup chopped sweet green pepper
½ cup sliced ripe olives
1¼ pints (2½ cups) Canned Tomatoes
1½ tablespoons chili powder
½ teaspoon garlic powder
¾ cup grated cheddar cheese

Preheat oven to 350°F.

Mix cornmeal with 1 cup cold water. Mix remaining 2 cups water and ½ teaspoon salt in a heavy saucepan with a lid; bring to a boil. Stir cornmeal into boiling water and cook over low heat, stirring until mixture thickens. Cover pan and cook over low heat for 10 minutes.

Heat oil in skillet. Add ground beef, green pepper, and ½ teaspoon salt; cook for about 5 minutes, stirring constantly. Add olives, tomatoes, chili powder, and garlic powder; simmer and stir for 5 minutes.

Line bottom and sides of a greased two-quart baking dish with cooked cornmeal. Spoon meat mixture over cornmeal. Sprinkle grated cheese over top.

Bake at 350°F for about 30 minutes.

Yield: 4 to 6 servings

NOTE: This casserole can be assembled and frozen before baking. Let casserole cool and wrap well before freezing. When ready to serve, thaw casserole and bake according to instructions.

Gertrude Filipovich, Abilene, Texas (West Texas Fair & Rodeo, Abilene, Texas)

Six-Layer Dinner

6 medium potatoes, peeled and sliced
2 pounds ground beef
½ teaspoon salt, divided
¼ teaspoon pepper
¼ teaspoon garlic powder
1 medium onion, sliced
1 pint (2 cups) Canned Carrots, drained
  and sliced
¾ cup uncooked rice, washed
½ pint (1 cup) Canned Tomato Juice
1 quart (4 cups) Canned Tomatoes

Preheat oven to 375°F.

Assemble ingredients in a small roasting pan in the following order: For first layer, arrange potatoes on bottom of pan. For second layer, mix raw ground beef with ¼ teaspoon salt, pepper, and garlic powder; crumble over potatoes. For third layer, arrange onion slices over ground beef. For fourth layer, place carrots on top of onions. For fifth layer, cover carrots with uncooked rice. For sixth layer, combine tomato juice and tomatoes with remaining ¼ teaspoon salt; pour evenly over top of assembled ingredients.

Cover and bake at 375°F for 1 hour 30 minutes.

Yield: 6 servings

NOTE: This dish can be assembled ahead of time and refrigerated. It is a great "make-and-take" dish.

Carolyn Lynch, Williston, North Dakota (Upper Missouri Valley Fair, Williston, North Dakota)

Tomatoes and Okra

½ pound bacon, diced
4 cups chopped okra
2 pints (4 cups) Canned Tomatoes
3 tablespoons soy sauce
4 teaspoons hot pepper sauce
1 cup chopped onion
1 clove garlic, chopped
2 tablespoons parsley flakes

Fry bacon in a large skillet until lightly browned. Add okra and continue frying for about 10 minutes. Add all remaining ingredients and mix well. Simmer, stirring occasionally, until onions are cooked (about 30 minutes).

Yield: 6 servings

NOTE: This can be served as a vegetable or over rice.

Martha Bell, Pryor, Oklahoma (Tulsa State Fair, Tulsa, Oklahoma)

Canned Tomato Juice

26 pounds firm, red-ripe tomatoes
Bottled lemon juice or citric acid
Salt (optional)
Sugar (optional)
Fruit preserver (optional)

Prepare home canning jars and lids according to manufacturer's instructions.

Wash and drain tomatoes. Remove blossom ends and cores; cut tomatoes into small pieces. Place tomatoes in a large saucepan and simmer over medium heat until soft, stirring frequently to prevent sticking. Press cooked tomatoes through a fine sieve or food mill. Add 2 tablespoons bottled lemon juice or ½ teaspoon citric acid to each quart. Place 1 teaspoon salt, ½ teaspoon sugar, and ½ teaspoon fruit preserver in each quart jar, if desired. Pour hot tomato juice into hot jars, leaving ¼-inch headspace. Adjust caps.

Process quarts 45 minutes in a boiling water bath canner.

Yield: about 7 quarts

Wanda Davis, New Hope, Kentucky (Nelson County Fair, Bardstown, Kentucky)

Peppy Tomato Juice

1 quart (4 cups) Canned Tomato Juice
1 small onion, chopped
4 teaspoons lemon juice
½ teaspoon salt
⅛ teaspoon black pepper

Combine tomato juice and onion; refrigerate until chilled. Strain tomato juice; discard onion. Add lemon juice, salt, and pepper to juice. Serve with cheese dip and crackers.

Yield: 8 servings

Alice Like, Murray, Kentucky (Murray-Calloway County Fair, Murray, Kentucky)

Zucchini Casserole

¾ pound ground beef
3 cups fine bread crumbs
4 tablespoons margarine, melted
1 (8 ounce) package American cheese slices
4 cups sliced zucchini
1 tablespoon oregano
1 medium onion, finely chopped
½ cup finely chopped sweet green pepper
Salt and pepper to taste
1 pint (2 cups) Canned Tomato Juice or Canned Spicy Tomato Sauce

Preheat oven to 350°F. Grease a 1½-quart casserole dish with butter or margarine; set aside.

Brown ground beef; drain well. Toast bread crumbs in margarine in a skillet; remove from heat and set aside. Cut cheese slices diagonally into triangles. Mix zucchini and oregano in a bowl. Using one-third of each, layer ingredients in casserole dish in the following order: zucchini, onion, ground beef, green pepper, cheese, bread crumbs, salt, pepper, and tomato juice. Repeat layers two more times, saving the bread crumbs from the third layer to sprinkle on top.

Cover and bake at 350°F for 45 minutes to 1 hour or until zucchini is tender.

Yield: 10 servings

NOTE: Ground beef may be omitted to make a vegetarian casserole.

Wanda Davis, New Hope, Kentucky (Nelson County Fair, Bardstown, Kentucky)

Canned Spicy Tomato Juice

21 pounds firm, ripe tomatoes
3 tablespoons seasoned salt
1 tablespoon Worcestershire sauce
1 tablespoon hot pepper sauce
 (optional)
Bottled lemon juice or citric acid

Wash, core, and quarter tomatoes. Extract juice from tomatoes using an electric juice extractor or by simmering until soft and pressing through a sieve or food mill.

Prepare home canning jars and lids according to manufacturer's instructions.

Pour tomato juice into a large saucepot; add seasoned salt, Worcestershire sauce, and hot pepper sauce. Heat juice to a simmer; do not boil. Add 2 tablespoons bottled lemon juice or ½ teaspoon citric acid to each quart. Pour hot tomato juice into hot jars, leaving ¼-inch headspace. Adjust caps.

Process quarts 45 minutes in a boiling water bath canner.

Yield: about 7 quarts

Ball Recipe

Gazpacho

6 medium tomatoes
2 medium cucumbers
1¼ quarts (5 cups) Canned Spicy Tomato
  Juice
1 medium onion, chopped
1 medium sweet green pepper, chopped
½ cup chopped celery
1 clove garlic, minced
½ cup wine vinegar
2 tablespoons olive oil
1 teaspoon salt
½ teaspoon hot pepper sauce
¼ teaspoon pepper
Croutons or shredded cheddar cheese
  (for garnish)

Peel, core, seed, and chop tomatoes. Peel, seed, and chop cucumbers. Combine all ingredients except croutons and shredded cheese; chill. Serve in chilled soup bowls; garnish with croutons or shredded cheddar cheese.

Yield: 10 to 12 servings

Ball Recipe

Canned Spicy Tomato Sauce

3 medium onions, finely chopped
2 cloves garlic, minced
3 tablespoons olive oil
10 pounds tomatoes, peeled and
   cored
1 tablespoon salt
1½ teaspoons oregano
1 teaspoon black pepper
1 teaspoon sugar

In a large saucepot, sauté onion and garlic in oil until tender; do not brown. Chop peeled and cored tomatoes in a food processor or blender. Add tomatoes and all remaining ingredients to mixture in saucepot; simmer about 2 hours, stirring occasionally.

Prepare home canning jars and lids according to manufacturer's instructions.

Put tomato mixture in a food mill and press out liquid and pulp. Discard seeds. Return liquid and pulp to saucepot; cook uncovered over medium-high heat until sauce thickens, stirring frequently to prevent sticking. Pour hot sauce into hot jars, leaving ¼-inch headspace. Adjust caps.

Process half-pints 30 minutes in a boiling water bath canner.

Yield: about 5 half-pints

Ball Recipe

Chicken Cacciatore

1 (2½ to 3 pounds) broiler-fryer chicken, cut up
2 tablespoons shortening
⅓ cup all-purpose flour
2 medium onions, sliced into thin rings
1 medium sweet green pepper, chopped
2 cloves garlic, crushed
1 pint (2 cups) Canned Tomatoes, drained
½ pint (1 cup) Canned Spicy Tomato Sauce
½ cup canned or fresh sliced mushrooms
1 teaspoon salt

Wash chicken and pat dry. Heat shortening in a large skillet. Coat chicken pieces with flour; fry in shortening over medium heat until browned (15 to 20 minutes). Remove chicken from pan and drain on paper towels; set aside.

Cook onion, green pepper, and garlic in remaining shortening until tender; stir in tomatoes, tomato sauce, mushrooms, and salt. Add chicken, cover pan, and simmer 30 to 40 minutes.

Yield: 4 to 5 servings

Ball Recipe

Canned Barbecue Sauce

10 pounds tomatoes, peeled and
   cored
2 cups chopped onion
3 cloves garlic, minced
1 tablespoon crushed red pepper
1 tablespoon celery seed
1½ cups brown sugar
1 cup vinegar
⅓ cup lemon juice
1 tablespoon dry mustard
2 teaspoons salt
1½ teaspoons mace
1 teaspoon ginger
1 teaspoon cinnamon

Chop tomatoes in a food processor
or blender. Combine tomatoes,
onion, garlic, red pepper, and
celery seed in a large saucepot;
cover and simmer until vegetables
are soft (about 30 minutes).

Prepare home canning jars and
lids according to manufacturer's
instructions.

Put tomato mixture in a food mill
and press out liquid and pulp.
Discard seeds. Return liquid and
pulp to saucepot; add all
remaining ingredients and cook
over low heat until mixture
thickens (about 30 minutes). Pour
hot sauce into hot jars, leaving ¼-
inch headspace. Adjust caps.

Process pints 20 minutes in a
boiling water bath canner.

Yield: about 3 pints

Ball Recipe

BBQ Hash

2 cups whole kernel corn (fresh or frozen),
  cooked and drained
2 cups diced cooked ham
3 medium red potatoes, cooked and
  cubed (do not peel)
½ cup sliced green onion
½ cup chopped sweet green pepper
½ pint (1 cup) Canned Barbecue Sauce
¼ cup (½ stick) butter or margarine
½ cup shredded cheddar cheese

Combine corn, ham, potatoes, onion, green pepper, and barbecue sauce in a mixing bowl; set aside. Melt butter or margarine in a large skillet over medium heat. Cook vegetable and ham mixture in butter 5 minutes or until bottom begins to brown. With a wide spatula, turn hash and continue cooking about 5 minutes. Top with cheese before serving.

Yield: 7 servings

Ball Recipe

Canned Chili Sauce

2½ quarts chopped red tomatoes
2 large onions, diced
3 hot peppers, diced (more or less, to taste)
2 sweet green peppers, diced
3½ cups sugar
2 tablespoons salt
½ teaspoon nutmeg
½ teaspoon cinnamon
½ teaspoon ground allspice
½ teaspoon black pepper
1 cup vinegar, 5% acidity

Prepare home canning jars and lids according to manufacturer's instructions.

Combine all ingredients in a large saucepan; mix well. Cover and simmer over moderate heat, stirring occasionally, until vegetables are tender. Remove lid and continue cooking until mixture begins to thicken slightly. (Total cooking time will be 2 to 2½ hours.) Do not overcook or cook too quickly. Pour hot sauce into hot jars, leaving ¼-inch headspace. Adjust caps.

Process pints 15 minutes in a boiling water bath canner.

Yield: about 7 pints

NOTE: When cutting or seeding hot peppers, wear rubber gloves to prevent burning of hands.

Helen V. Cameron, Pine Bluff, Arkansas (Southeast Arkansas District Fair, Pine Bluff, Arkansas)

Canned Chili Sauce

4½ cups vinegar, 5% acidity
2 tablespoons whole cloves
3 cinnamon sticks, broken in half
1 tablespoon celery seed
1 tablespoon whole allspice
15 pounds tomatoes
3 cups sugar, divided
½ cup chopped onion
½ teaspoon cayenne pepper
2 tablespoons salt

Prepare home canning jars and lids according to manufacturer's instructions.

Combine vinegar, cloves, cinnamon sticks, celery seed, and allspice; bring to a boil. Remove from heat and set aside. Peel and chop tomatoes. Combine half of the tomatoes, 1½ cups sugar, onion, and cayenne pepper in a large saucepot; bring to a boil. Simmer 40 minutes, stirring frequently. Stir in remaining tomatoes and sugar; boil 40 minutes, stirring frequently. Strain vinegar mixture; discard spices. Add vinegar and salt to tomato mixture; cook about 30 minutes or until desired consistency is reached. Pour hot sauce into hot jars, leaving ¼-inch headspace. Adjust caps.

Process pints 15 minutes in a boiling water bath canner.

Yield: about 6 pints

Ball Recipe

Salisbury Steak

1½ pounds ground beef
¾ cup quick-cooking rolled oats
  (uncooked)
¼ cup chopped onion
2 teaspoons salt
¼ teaspoon pepper
1 egg
¼ pint (½ cup) Canned Tomato Juice
¼ pint (½ cup) Canned Chili Sauce (Ball
  Recipe)
6 bacon slices

Preheat oven to 375°F.

Combine all ingredients except bacon; mix thoroughly. Divide mixture into six equal portions; shape each portion into a patty about 1½ inches thick. Wrap a slice of bacon around each patty; secure with toothpicks.

Bake at 375°F for 45 to 50 minutes.

Yield: 6 servings

NOTE: Ground turkey can be used in place of ground beef.

Bonnie Groh, East Aurora, New York (Erie County Fair & Expo, Hamburg, New York)

Sloppy Joes

1½ pounds ground beef
¾ cup diced onion
1 clove garlic, minced
⅓ cup brown sugar
1 tablespoon prepared mustard
¼ pint (½ cup) Canned Tomato Ketchup
½ pint (1 cup) Canned Chili Sauce
  (Southeast Arkansas District Fair Recipe)
¼ cup water
2 tablespoons Worcestershire sauce
1 tablespoon lemon juice
½ teaspoon salt
¼ teaspoon thyme

In a large saucepot, brown ground beef, onion, and garlic. Drain off fat; set beef mixture aside. Combine brown sugar and mustard; add all remaining ingredients and mix well. Add sauce to beef mixture, mixing well. Heat thoroughly. Serve on buns.

Yield: 6 servings

Ball Recipe

Canned Pizza Sauce

3 medium onions, finely chopped
4 cloves garlic, minced
3 tablespoons olive oil
10 pounds tomatoes, cored and
    quartered
1 tablespoon each: basil, oregano
    and Italian seasoning
1 teaspoon salt
1 teaspoon crushed red pepper
1 teaspoon black pepper
1 teaspoon sugar

Prepare home canning jars and lids according to manufacturer's instructions.

In a large saucepot, sauté onion and garlic in oil until tender. Add all remaining ingredients and simmer 2 hours, stirring occasionally. Press mixture through a food mill. Discard seeds and peel. Return juice and pulp to saucepot; cook uncovered over medium-high heat until sauce thickens, stirring frequently to prevent sticking. Pour hot sauce into hot jars, leaving ¼-inch headspace. Adjust caps.

Process pints 30 minutes in a boiling water bath canner.

Yield: about 4 pints

Ball Recipe

Pizza Puffs

2 (10 count) packages refrigerator biscuits
½ pint (1 cup) Canned Pizza Sauce
40 thin slices pepperoni
20 (½-inch) cubes mozzarella cheese
1 egg, beaten
¼ cup grated Parmesan cheese

Preheat oven to 375°F.

Separate biscuits and flatten with the palm of your hand, making each three to four inches in diameter. Brush each biscuit with pizza sauce. Place 2 slices of pepperoni in the center of each biscuit; top with a cube of mozzarella cheese. Fold edges of biscuit to center and pinch to seal. Place on greased baking sheet, seam side down. Brush tops with egg and sprinkle with Parmesan cheese.

Bake at 375°F for 15 minutes.

Yield: 20 pizza puffs

Ball Recipe

Canned Spaghetti Sauce

3 medium onions, finely chopped
4 cloves garlic, minced
3 tablespoons olive oil
10 pounds tomatoes, peeled and
  cored
2 sweet green peppers, finely
  chopped
2 tablespoons each: basil, oregano
  and Italian seasoning
1 tablespoon salt
1 teaspoon pepper

Prepare home canning jars and lids according to manufacturer's instructions.

In a large saucepot, sauté onion and garlic in oil until tender. Add all remaining ingredients and simmer about 1 hour, stirring occasionally. Press mixture through a food mill. Discard seeds and peel. Return juice and pulp to saucepot; cook over medium heat until sauce thickens, stirring frequently to prevent sticking. Pour hot sauce into hot jars, leaving ¼-inch headspace. Adjust caps.

Process pints 30 minutes in a boiling water bath canner.

Yield: about 4 pints

Ball Recipe

Busy Day Casserole

(Microwave Recipe)

1 pound ground beef
1 pint (2 cups) Canned Spaghetti Sauce
1 cup water
1½ cups elbow macaroni (uncooked)
1 cup shredded mozzarella cheese

Crumble ground beef into a three-quart casserole. Microwave on High 4 to 5 minutes or until ground beef is no longer pink; stir or rotate halfway through cooking time. Add spaghetti sauce, water, and macaroni; mix well. Cover and microwave on High 12 to 14 minutes or until macaroni is tender; stir or rotate halfway through cooking time. Remove from microwave oven and sprinkle with shredded cheese. Cover casserole and let stand 4 to 6 minutes before serving.

Yield: 6 servings

Vyla Blough, Waterloo, Iowa (National Cattle Congress Exposition, Waterloo, Iowa)

Canned Tomato Ketchup

24 large red-ripe tomatoes, peeled
    and chopped (4 quarts)
1 cup chopped onion
½ cup chopped sweet red pepper
1½ teaspoons celery seed
1 teaspoon whole allspice
1 teaspoon mustard seed
1 cinnamon stick
1 cup sugar
1 tablespoon salt
1 tablespoon paprika
1½ cups vinegar, 5% acidity

Prepare home canning jars and lids according to manufacturer's instructions.

Combine tomatoes, onion, and pepper in a saucepan; cook until vegetables are soft. Press vegetables through a food mill or sieve. Return liquid and pulp to saucepan and cook rapidly until thick. (This will take about 4 to 5 hours until the volume is reduced by more than half.)

Tie whole spices in a cheesecloth bag; add with sugar and salt to tomato mixture. Cook about 25 minutes, stirring often. Add paprika and vinegar; cook until thick. Discard spice bag. Pour hot ketchup into hot jars, leaving ¼-inch headspace. Adjust caps.

Process pints 10 minutes in a boiling water bath canner.

Yield: about 3 pints

Claudia Davis, Hayden Lake, Idaho (North Idaho Fair, Coeur d'Alene, Idaho)

Blue-Ribbon Meat Loaf

1½ pounds ground beef
¾ cup old-fashioned rolled oats
　　(uncooked)
4 teaspoons chopped onion
1 teaspoon salt
¼ teaspoon pepper
1 teaspoon parsley flakes
1 egg, beaten
½ pint (1 cup) Canned Tomato Ketchup

Preheat oven to 350°F.

Mix all ingredients until well blended. Shape mixture into a meat loaf about ten inches long and three inches thick.

Bake at 350°F for approximately 1 hour 15 minutes. Let stand about 15 minutes before serving.

Yield: 6 servings

NOTE: Ground turkey can be used in place of ground beef.

Claudia Davis, Hayden Lake, Idaho (North Idaho Fair, Coeur d'Alene, Idaho)

Canned Spicy Tomato Ketchup

12 pounds ripe tomatoes
2 large onions
1 sweet red pepper, seeded
1 tablespoon mustard seed
1 tablespoon black peppercorns
2 teaspoons whole allspice
1 whole cinnamon stick
1 tablespoon dry basil
1 large bay leaf
2 small dried hot chili peppers
1½ cups firmly packed brown
    sugar
1 tablespoon salt
1 tablespoon paprika
1 cup vinegar, 5% acidity

Prepare home canning jars and lids according to manufacturer's instructions.

Cut tomatoes, onions, and red pepper into pieces; place in a blender or food processor container and process until smooth. Press mixture through a wire strainer. Measure 6 quarts of purée into a ten-quart pot; bring to a boil over medium-high heat. Boil gently, uncovered and stirring often, until reduced by half (about 1 hour). Tie whole spices and chili peppers in a cheesecloth bag; add to purée. Add brown sugar, salt, and paprika, stirring until well blended; continue boiling until mixture is very thick (about 1½ to 2 hours). As mixture thickens, reduce heat to prevent sticking. Add vinegar during last 10 to 15 minutes of boiling. Remove from heat. Discard spice bag. Pour hot ketchup into hot jars, leaving ¼-inch headspace. Adjust caps.

Process pints 10 minutes in a boiling water bath canner.

Yield: about 4 pints

Warren L. Knudtson, Las Vegas, Nevada (Las Vegas Jaycees State Fair, Las Vegas, Nevada)

PICKLES & RELISHES

PICKLES & RELISHES

Pickled Baby Beets

3 cups white vinegar, 5%
   acidity
1 cup water
1½ pounds dark brown
   sugar
¼ teaspoon salt
2 tablespoons mustard seed
1 tablespoon celery seed
1 teaspoon cloves
1 teaspoon allspice
½ teaspoon cinnamon
5 dozen baby beets, cooked
   and skinned

Prepare home canning jars and lids according to manufacturer's instructions.

Mix vinegar, water, brown sugar, and salt in a large kettle. Tie all spices in a cheesecloth bag; add to vinegar mixture, stirring well. Bring mixture to a boil; boil 5 minutes. Add beets to hot liquid; simmer 5 minutes. Discard spice bag.

Pack hot beets into hot jars, leaving ¼-inch headspace. Pour hot liquid over beets, leaving ¼-inch headspace. Remove air bubbles with a non-metallic spatula. Adjust caps.

Process pints 30 minutes in a boiling water bath canner.

Yield: about 6 pints

NOTE: Use baby beets so they can be canned whole. Do not cut beet tops shorter than two inches before boiling beets—otherwise beets will bleed and centers will be white.

Mary Looker Pfremmer, Smith River, California (California State Grange Fair, Sacramento, California)

Pickled Beets

2 gallons beets, freshly dug
  and trimmed
5 cups white vinegar, 5%
  acidity
5 cups water
2 pounds brown sugar
2 tablespoons salt

Prepare home canning jars and lids according to manufacturer's instructions.

Dig beets the same day they are to be processed. Wash beets thoroughly, being careful not to scratch the skins. Cut off leaves and tops of stems, leaving one inch of the stem. Do not cut off "tails." Sort beets according to size and keep them sorted throughout the entire canning process.

Bring a large pot of water to a rolling boil; add beets, one size group at a time. Boil until the skins will come off easily. Put beets in cold water, then remove skins, tops, and "tails." Trim beets if necessary. There is no need to cool beets completely. Do not soak beets. Pack beets into hot jars, leaving ¼-inch headspace. Cut beets, if necessary, to have all beets in a jar the same size.

In another large pot, combine vinegar, water, brown sugar, and salt; bring to a boil. Pour hot liquid over beets, leaving ¼-inch headspace. Make sure all beets are covered by liquid. Remove air bubbles with a non-metallic spatula. Adjust caps.

Process pints 30 minutes in a boiling water bath canner.

Yield: about 15 pints

Rebecca Christensen, Blackfoot, Idaho (Eastern Idaho State Fair, Blackfoot, Idaho)

Sweet Pickled Beets

9 pounds small, young beets
2 cups sugar
2 cups water
2 cups vinegar, 5% acidity
1 tablespoon cinnamon
1 teaspoon cloves
1 teaspoon allspice

Prepare home canning jars and lids according to manufacturer's instructions.

Wash beets. Trim off tops, leaving three inches of the stem; do not cut off roots. Boil beets until skins will slip off easily (about 15 minutes). While beets are cooking, combine sugar, water, vinegar, cinnamon, cloves, and allspice in a large saucepan; bring to a boil.

Put cooked beets in cold water. Remove skins and cut off tops and roots. Pack beets into hot jars, leaving ¼-inch headspace. Pour hot liquid over beets, leaving ¼-inch headspace. Remove air bubbles with a non-metallic spatula. Adjust caps.

Process pints 30 minutes in a boiling water bath canner.

Yield: about 6 pints

NOTE: For sweeter pickles, add ¼ cup sugar; for more tartness, add ¼ cup vinegar.

Dixie Peterson, Caliente, Nevada (Las Vegas Jaycees State Fair, Las Vegas, Nevada)

Bread and Butter Pickles

5 quarts thinly sliced
  cucumbers
8 medium onions, sliced
2 sweet green peppers,
  chopped
2 sweet red peppers,
  chopped
½ cup canning salt
Ice cubes
5 cups white vinegar, 5%
  acidity
5 cups sugar
2 tablespoons mustard seed
1½ teaspoons turmeric
1 teaspoon celery seed
½ teaspoon cloves

Prepare home canning jars and lids according to manufacturer's instructions.

Combine cucumbers, onions, green and red peppers, and salt; mix well. Cover vegetables with ice cubes and let stand 2 hours. Drain vegetables thoroughly; pat dry with paper towels.

Combine vinegar, sugar, and spices in a large saucepan; bring to a boil. Add drained vegetables and slowly bring to a boil; boil 5 minutes. Pack hot mixture into hot jars, leaving ¼-inch headspace. Remove air bubbles with a non-metallic spatula. Adjust caps.

Process pints 10 minutes in a boiling water bath canner.

Yield: about 10 pints

Bonnie Groh, East Aurora, New York (Erie County Fair & Expo, Hamburg, New York)

Bread and Butter Pickles

4 pounds cucumbers, thinly
  sliced (4 to 6 inch cucumbers)
2 pounds onions, thinly sliced
  (about 8 small onions)
⅓ cup canning salt
Ice cubes
3 cups vinegar, 5% acidity
2 cups sugar
2 teaspoons turmeric
2 teaspoons celery seed
1 teaspoon ginger
1 teaspoon peppercorns

Prepare home canning jars and lids according to manufacturer's instructions.

Combine cucumber and onion slices in a large bowl; layer with salt and cover with ice cubes. Let stand 1½ hours. Drain and rinse.

Combine vinegar, sugar, and spices in a large saucepan; bring to a boil. Add drained vegetables and bring to a boil. Pack hot mixture into hot jars, leaving ¼-inch headspace. Remove air bubbles with a non-metallic spatula. Adjust caps.

Process pints 10 minutes in a boiling water bath canner.

Yield: about 7 pints

NOTE: If you tie the spices in cheesecloth or place them in a tea ball, a layer of spices will not settle in the bottom of the jars.

*Debi Mosier, Sperry, Oklahoma
(Tulsa State Fair, Tulsa,
Oklahoma)*

Chicken Cheese Rolls

1 cup chopped cooked chicken
1 cup diced cheddar cheese
3 hard-cooked eggs, chopped
2 tablespoons chopped stuffed green olives
2 tablespoons chopped Bread and Butter
   Pickles
2 tablespoons chopped onion
2 tablespoons chopped sweet green pepper
½ cup mayonnaise (or to taste)
6 hot dog buns

Preheat oven to 325°F.

Combine all ingredients except buns in a bowl; mix well. Divide chicken mixture into six equal portions; spoon into hot dog buns. Wrap buns in foil.

Bake at 325°F for 25 minutes.

Yield: 6 servings

NOTE: In place of chicken, you can use ground turkey that has been browned or leftover baked turkey. Swiss cheese can be used in place of cheddar.

Debi Mosier, Sperry, Oklahoma (Tulsa State Fair, Tulsa, Oklahoma)

Zucchini Bread and Butter Pickles

6 pounds zucchini (7 to 10
  inches long, 1 inch in
  diameter)
1½ cups chopped onion
  (about 1 pound onions;
  use sweet onions such as
  Bermudas)
2 large cloves garlic
⅓ cup canning salt
2 quarts crushed ice cubes
  (2 trays)
4½ cups sugar
2 tablespoons mustard seed
1½ teaspoons turmeric
1½ teaspoons celery seed
3 cups white vinegar, 5%
  acidity

Wash zucchini; do not peel. Cut zucchini into ¼-inch slices; discard the ends. Combine 4 cups sliced zucchini with onion and garlic; add salt and mix thoroughly. Cover vegetables with ice and refrigerate 3 hours.

Prepare home canning jars and lids according to manufacturer's instructions.

Drain vegetables thoroughly. Discard garlic. Combine sugar, spices, and vinegar in a saucepan; heat just to boiling. Add drained vegetables and heat 5 minutes. Pack hot mixture loosely into hot jars, leaving ¼-inch headspace. Cover with hot liquid, leaving ¼-inch headspace. Remove air bubbles with a non-metallic spatula. Adjust caps.

Process pints 10 minutes in a boiling water bath canner.

Yield: about 7 pints

Cathy Grant, Wasilla, Alaska
(Alaska State Fair, Palmer, Alaska)

Crystal Pickles

4 large cucumbers, thinly sliced
5 small onions, thinly sliced
1 large sweet green pepper, thinly
  sliced
1 large clove garlic
¼ cup canning salt
2 quarts cold water
14 ice cubes
3½ cups sugar
1½ cups white vinegar, 5%
  acidity
1 tablespoon mustard seed
1 teaspoon celery seed
1 teaspoon turmeric

Prepare home canning jars and lids according to manufacturer's instructions.

Combine cucumbers, onions, and green pepper; add garlic clove wrapped in cheesecloth. Mix salt with cold water and pour over vegetables. Cover with ice cubes and let stand 2 hours. Drain vegetables. Discard garlic clove.

Combine sugar, vinegar, mustard seed, celery seed, and turmeric in a large saucepan; bring to a boil. Add drained vegetables and bring mixture almost to a boil, but do not boil. Pack hot mixture into hot jars, leaving ¼-inch headspace. Remove air bubbles with a non-metallic spatula. Adjust caps.

Process pints 10 minutes in a boiling water bath canner.

Yield: about 3 pints

Lillie Harper, Haynesville, Louisiana (Claiborne Parish Fair, Haynesville, Louisiana)

Ham-and-Cheese Sandwich Spread

1 cup finely chopped cooked ham
1 cup shredded Swiss cheese
⅓ cup chopped Crystal Pickles
⅓ cup mayonnaise
1 tablespoon minced onion

Combine all ingredients in a bowl and mix thoroughly. Store covered in refrigerator.

Yield: 8 servings

Ball Recipe

Delicious Dills

Green grape leaves
3 pounds cucumbers (4 to 5
    inches long)
8 heads and stems of dill
2 teaspoons ground horseradish
2 teaspoons mustard seed
2 cloves garlic
3 cups water
2½ cups vinegar, 5% acidity
⅓ cup canning salt

Prepare home canning jars and lids according to manufacturer's instructions.

Line bottoms of hot jars with grape leaves. Wash cucumbers. Cut cucumbers in half lengthwise and pack into hot jars, leaving ¼-inch headspace. Divide dill, horseradish, mustard seed, and garlic equally among the jars. Combine water, vinegar, and salt in a saucepan; bring to a boil. Pour hot liquid over cucumbers, leaving ¼-inch headspace. Remove air bubbles with a non-metallic spatula. Adjust caps.

Process quarts 15 minutes in a boiling water bath canner.

Yield: about 2 quarts

NOTE: Do not open jars for at least two weeks so flavor will have a chance to develop.

Allison Williams, Scottsdale, Arizona (Arizona State Fair, Phoenix, Arizona)

Dill Pickles

12 pounds freshly picked
   cucumbers (4 to 6 inches long)
1 medium head of dill per quart
2 medium cloves of garlic per
   quart
3 quarts water
6 cups apple cider vinegar, 5%
   acidity
1 cup canning salt

Prepare home canning jars and lids according to manufacturer's instructions.

Wash and drain cucumbers. Place one head of dill in the bottom of each hot jar. Add 2 cloves of garlic to each jar. Pack cucumbers into hot jars, leaving ¼-inch headspace. Combine water, vinegar, and salt, stirring until salt dissolves; heat to boiling. Pour hot liquid over cucumbers, leaving ¼-inch headspace. Remove air bubbles with a non-metallic spatula. Adjust caps.

Process quarts 15 minutes in a boiling water bath canner.

Yield: about 6 quarts

NOTE: For the best flavor, do not open jars for four weeks. Save unused liquid until more cucumbers are available for pickling.

Thelma Meyer, Bella Vista, California (California State Grange Fair, Sacramento, California)

Kosher Dill Pickles

20 to 25 freshly picked cucumbers
   (4 inches long)
3 to 4 cloves garlic
3 to 4 heads of dill
3 to 4 hot red peppers
6 cups cider vinegar, 5% acidity
1 cup canning salt
3 quarts water

Prepare home canning jars and lids according to manufacturer's instructions.

Wash cucumbers thoroughly. Cover cucumbers with cold water and let stand about 1 hour. Remove cucumbers from water and wipe dry. Pack cucumbers into hot jars, leaving ¼-inch headspace. To each quart, add 1 clove garlic, 1 head dill, and 1 (whole) hot red pepper. Combine vinegar, salt, and water in a saucepan; bring to a boil. Pour hot liquid over cucumbers, leaving ¼-inch headspace. Remove air bubbles with a non-metallic spatula. Adjust caps.

Process pints 15 minutes in a boiling water bath canner.

Yield: about 4 pints

*Nola J. Michael, Laurel, Montana
(MontanaFair, Billings, Montana)*

Kosher Dill Pickles

2 pounds fresh pickling
 cucumbers per quart (3 to 4
 inches long)
2 to 3 cloves fresh garlic per quart
2 heads fresh dill per quart
1 to 2 small dried hot peppers per
 quart
6 cups cider vinegar, 5% acidity
¾ cup canning salt
3 quarts cold water

Prepare home canning jars and
lids according to manufacturer's
instructions.

Wash and gently scrub
cucumbers. Pack cucumbers into
hot jars, leaving ¼-inch
headspace. Add garlic, dill, and
peppers to jars. Mix vinegar, salt,
and water in a large saucepot;
bring to a boil. Pour hot liquid
over cucumbers, leaving ¼-inch
headspace. Remove air bubbles
with a non-metallic spatula.
Adjust caps.

Process quarts 15 minutes in a
boiling water bath canner.

NOTE: Brine made according to
above recipe will cover eight to
ten quarts of pickles.

*Norma Wright, Albuquerque, New
Mexico (New Mexico State Fair,
Albuquerque, New Mexico)*

Sour Dill Pickles

35 to 40 medium cucumbers
  (leave whole)
Ice cubes
½ cup canning salt
1 quart vinegar, 5% acidity
1 quart water
3 tablespoons mixed pickling
  spice
7 heads of dill (one per jar)
7 cloves of garlic (one per jar)

Scrub freshly picked cucumbers; rinse. Combine cucumbers and ice cubes in a large pan; spread a layer of ice cubes over top. Cover pan and let stand about 2 hours. (This makes the pickles crisp.)

Prepare home canning jars and lids according to manufacturer's instructions.

Drain cucumbers; dry each cucumber. Combine salt, vinegar, and water in a saucepan. Tie pickling spice in a cheesecloth bag and add to vinegar mixture; simmer 15 minutes. Discard spice bag. Place one head of dill and one clove of garlic in each jar. Pack cucumbers into hot jars, packing closely and leaving ¼-inch headspace. Pour hot liquid over cucumbers, leaving ¼-inch headspace. Remove air bubbles with a non-metallic spatula. Adjust caps.

Process pints 15 minutes in a boiling water bath canner.

Yield: about 7 pints

Marguerite W. Barford, Augusta, West Virginia (Hampshire County Fair, Augusta, West Virginia)

Sour Dill Hors d'Oeuvres

1 (8 ounce) package cream cheese, softened
1 (6 ounce) package Italian salad dressing mix
1 loaf party rye bread, sliced
4 medium Sour Dill Pickles, sliced

Combine cream cheese with Italian salad dressing mix, stirring until well blended. Spread cream cheese on slices of bread; top with dill pickle slices. Cover and refrigerate until ready to serve.

Yield: 15 servings

Marguerite W. Barford, Augusta, West Virginia (Hampshire County Fair, Augusta, West Virginia)

Sweet Chunk Pickles

20 medium-size cucumbers (leave
   whole)
Boiling water
7 cups white sugar
5 teaspoons canning salt
2 tablespoons mixed pickling
   spice
4 cups vinegar, 5% acidity
Green food coloring (optional)

Wash cucumbers. Cover cucumbers with boiling water and let stand overnight. The next morning, drain and cover again with boiling water. Repeat this process for three mornings. On the fourth morning, drain cucumbers and cut into ½-inch pieces. Combine sugar, salt, pickling spice, and vinegar in a saucepan; bring to a boil. Pour hot liquid over cucumbers and let stand 2 days.

Prepare home canning jars and lids according to manufacturer's instructions.

Drain cucumbers, reserving liquid. Pack cucumbers into hot jars, leaving ¼-inch headspace. Bring pickling liquid to a boil; add food coloring, if desired. Pour hot liquid over cucumbers, leaving ¼-inch headspace. Remove air bubbles with a non-metallic spatula. Adjust caps.

Process pints 15 minutes in a boiling water bath canner.

Yield: about 6 pints

NOTE: Adding green food coloring makes an attractive jar of pickles.

Donna Mae Dragseth, Alamo, North Dakota (Upper Missouri Valley Fair, Williston, North Dakota)

Tuna Burgers

1 (6½ ounce) can tuna, drained
¾ cup shredded Swiss cheese
¾ cup ketchup
½ cup chopped celery
½ cup chopped Sweet Chunk Pickles,
   drained
2 tablespoons chopped onion
5 hamburger buns

Preheat oven to 375°F.

Combine all ingredients except buns in a bowl; mix well. Divide mixture into five equal portions; spread on hamburger buns. Wrap each sandwich in aluminum foil.

Bake at 375°F for 15 to 20 minutes.

Yield: 5 servings

Ball Recipe

Peach Pickles

8 pounds peaches
6¾ cups sugar
1 quart apple cider vinegar, 5% acidity
4 sticks cinnamon
2 tablespoons whole cloves

Wash and peel peaches. Place peaches in soaking solution to prevent darkening. Combine sugar and vinegar in a saucepan; boil 5 minutes. Tie cinnamon and cloves in a cheesecloth bag and add to hot liquid. Drain peaches and add to hot liquid; cook 5 minutes. Remove saucepan from heat; let peaches sit in syrup overnight to plump.

Prepare home canning jars and lids according to manufacturer's instructions.

Bring peaches and syrup to a boil. Discard spice bag. Pack hot peaches into hot jars, leaving ¼-inch headspace. Pour hot syrup over peaches, leaving ¼-inch headspace. Remove air bubbles with a non-metallic spatula. Adjust caps.

Process pints 20 minutes in a boiling water bath canner.

Yield: about 6 pints

NOTE: These peaches are especially good with baked ham.

Estelle W. Bragg, Vienna, Georgia (Central Georgia Fair, Cordele, Georgia)

Hungarian Peppers

4 quarts firm, fresh Hungarian
   peppers
½ cup canning salt
1 quart water
1 tablespoon sugar
1½ teaspoons prepared
   horseradish
1 small clove garlic
2½ cups vinegar, 5% acidity
½ cup water

When preparing peppers, protect your hands by wearing rubber gloves. Wash peppers; cut two small slits in each pepper. Leave petal and short stem intact. Dissolve salt in 1 quart water; pour over peppers and let stand in a cool place at least 12 hours.

Prepare home canning jars and lids according to manufacturer's instructions.

Drain peppers; rinse with clear water and drain again. Combine sugar, horseradish, garlic, vinegar, and ½ cup water in a saucepan; simmer 15 minutes. Discard garlic. Pack peppers into hot jars, leaving ¼-inch headspace. Pour hot liquid over peppers, leaving ¼-inch headspace. Remove air bubbles with a non-metallic spatula. Adjust caps.

Process pints 10 minutes in a boiling water bath canner.

Yield: about 8 pints

NOTE: Peppers may be used straight from the jar. Serve with any meat dish, with cold cuts, with vegetable or pasta salads, and of course, with Mexican dishes. These peppers make attractive gifts. Include one or two red or orange peppers in each jar. For jars to be used as gifts, you may want to strain liquid through a fine sieve to remove horseradish particles.

Wini Whitaker, Redmond, Oregon (Oregon State Fair, Salem, Oregon)

Cranberry-Pineapple Relish

1 (20 ounce) can crushed
  pineapple in its own juice
¾ cup sugar
5 thin lemon slices, chopped
5 thin orange slices, chopped
1 cinnamon stick
1 (12 ounce) package cranberries,
  chopped in food processor

Prepare home canning jars and lids according to manufacturer's instructions.

Combine pineapple, sugar, lemon, orange, and cinnamon stick in a small saucepan; heat until simmering. Cook 5 minutes or until syrupy. Add chopped cranberries and bring mixture to a boil. Remove from heat. Discard cinnamon stick. Pack hot relish into hot jars, leaving ¼-inch headspace. Adjust caps.

Process half-pints 15 minutes in a boiling water bath canner.

Yield: about 3 half-pints

NOTE: This is a wonderful condiment to serve with your holiday turkey.

Anna Marie Davis, Fair Oaks, California (California State Fair, Sacramento, California)

Cranberry-Pineapple Pastry

1 sheet frozen puff pastry, thawed (half of a
  17¼ ounce package)
½ cup Cranberry-Pineapple Relish
1 egg, slightly beaten
¾ cup confectioners' sugar
1 to 2 tablespoons boiling water

Cut pastry into thirds lengthwise, cutting along the folds. Place one third on top of another third; wrap in plastic wrap and refrigerate. On a lightly floured pastry board, roll remaining third into a 15x5-inch rectangle, then transfer to an ungreased cookie sheet. Chill.

With a pastry brush that has been dipped in water, moisten a one-inch border around all four edges of the dough on the cookie sheet. Spread relish on dough inside the moistened one-inch borders. Return to refrigerator.

Place the double layers of pastry on a pastry board and roll into a 15x5-inch rectangle. Fold in half lengthwise; using a small knife, cut one-inch crosswise slits one inch apart through the folded edge. Place the folded pastry on top of the chilled bottom layer; unfold top pastry. Press edges of pastry lightly; trim with a small, sharp knife. Brush top with egg; prick with a fork in several places. Chill 30 minutes.

Preheat oven to 400°F.

Bake pastry in the middle of the oven at 400°F for 1 minute. Reduce heat to 350°F and bake 35 minutes or until golden brown. Mix confectioners' sugar with enough boiling water to make a smooth glaze; drizzle glaze over hot pastry. Slide pastry from cookie sheet onto a rack to cool completely. Slice crosswise to serve.

Yield: 8 servings

NOTE: This relish is a wonderful blending of cranberries, pineapple, and citrus—and it is not too sweet.

Anna Marie Davis, Fair Oaks, California (California State Fair, Sacramento, California)

Pear Relish

18 pears
8 sweet green peppers
4 sweet red peppers
2 hot peppers
6 large onions
3 tablespoons mustard seed
1 tablespoon turmeric
1 teaspoon ginger
1 teaspoon cinnamon
1 teaspoon allspice
6 cups vinegar, 5% acidity
6 cups sugar

Prepare home canning jars and lids according to manufacturer's instructions.

Grind pears, peppers, and onions. Tie spices in a cheesecloth bag. Mix vinegar and sugar in a large saucepan; add spice bag and bring to a boil. Add ground pears, peppers, and onions; return to a boil. Simmer until mixture is thick (about 40 minutes), stirring constantly. Discard spice bag. Pack hot relish into hot jars, leaving ¼-inch headspace. Adjust caps.

Process pints 20 minutes in a boiling water bath canner.

Yield: about 6 pints

NOTE: When cutting or seeding hot peppers, wear rubber gloves to prevent burning of hands.

Alma L. Crawford, Lumpkin, Georgia (Chattahoochee Valley Fair, Columbus, Georgia)

Big Momma's Pear Relish

13 pounds pears, peeled and
  cored
5 sweet green peppers
3 sweet red peppers
3 hot peppers
5 large onions
5 cups sugar
1 teaspoon salt
5 cups vinegar, 5% acidity

Prepare home canning jars and lids according to manufacturer's instructions.

Grind pears using a food chopper. Grind peppers and onions. Combine all ingredients in a large cooking pot and bring to a boil. Cook 20 to 25 minutes or until mixture is no longer watery, stirring frequently. Pack hot relish into hot jars, leaving ¼-inch headspace. Adjust caps.

Process pints 20 minutes in a boiling water bath canner.

Yield: about 8 pints

NOTE: This relish is delicious on hot dogs or with dried pea soup. When cutting or seeding hot peppers, wear rubber gloves to prevent burning of hands.

Bonnye Bodiford, Montgomery, Alabama (South Alabama State Fair, Montgomery, Alabama)

Festive Pepper Relish

8 large sweet green peppers
8 large sweet red peppers
8 large sweet yellow peppers
8 large sweet onions
3 tablespoons salt
1 cup sugar
2 cups cider vinegar, 5% acidity
2 tablespoons Worcestershire
  sauce

Prepare home canning jars and lids according to manufacturer's instructions.

Wash peppers; remove seeds and pith. Grind peppers with coarse blade of food chopper. Peel onions, then grind. Combine peppers and onions in a large, heavy-bottomed cooking pot; sprinkle with salt and mix thoroughly. Add sugar, vinegar, and Worcestershire sauce; mix well. Simmer 20 minutes. Pack hot relish into hot jars, leaving 1/4-inch headspace. Adjust caps.

Process pints 15 minutes in a boiling water bath canner.

Yield: about 5 pints

NOTE: If yellow peppers are not available, you may use 12 red and 12 green peppers—although this combination will not be as colorful.

Terry Swann, Selbyville, Delaware (Delaware State Fair, Harrington, Delaware)

Sweet Pickle Relish

4 cups chopped cucumbers
2 cups chopped onions
1 sweet green pepper, chopped
1 sweet red pepper, chopped
¼ cup salt
3½ cups sugar
1 tablespoon celery seed
1 tablespoon mustard seed
2 cups cider vinegar, 5% acidity

Combine cucumbers, onions, and peppers in a large bowl; sprinkle with salt. Cover with cold water and let stand 2 hours.

Prepare home canning jars and lids according to manufacturer's instructions.

Drain vegetables thoroughly; press out liquid. Combine sugar, celery seed, mustard seed, and vinegar in a large saucepan; bring to a boil. Add drained vegetables and simmer 10 minutes. Pack hot relish into hot jars, leaving ¼-inch headspace. Adjust caps.

Process pints 10 minutes in a boiling water bath canner.

Yield: about 4 pints

Elinore L. Muccianti, Fresno, California (The Big Fresno Fair, Fresno, California)

Corned Beef Sandwich Spread

1 (12 ounce) can corned beef
¾ cup chopped celery
¼ cup Sweet Pickle Relish
⅓ cup mayonnaise
2 tablespoons minced onion
⅛ teaspoon garlic salt
⅛ teaspoon black pepper

Empty corned beef into a bowl and break up with a fork. Combine all remaining ingredients with corned beef; mix well. Cover and store in refrigerator.

Yield: 10 servings

Ball Recipe

Chicken Salad

½ baked chicken
¼ cup Pickle Relish
⅓ cup mayonnaise

Remove bones from chicken; chop chicken meat with a food chopper. Add relish and mayonnaise; mix well. Serve as a sandwich spread or as a dip for chips and crackers.

Yield: 6 to 8 servings

Vicki Shook, Wichita, Kansas (Kansas State Fair, Hutchinson, Kansas)

Pickle Relish

10 to 15 pounds cucumbers
2 large onions
4 sweet green peppers
1 sweet red pepper (for color)
½ cup salt
6 cups sugar
1 quart cider vinegar, 5% acidity
1 tablespoon mustard seed
1 tablespoon celery seed
½ teaspoon whole cloves
6 bay leaves

Wash vegetables. Cut off ends of cucumbers. Peel onions. Remove seeds from peppers. Chop all vegetables using a food chopper. Combine chopped vegetables in a pan or bowl; add salt and stir. Let stand about 1 hour.

Prepare home canning jars and lids according to manufacturer's instructions.

Drain vegetables. Combine drained vegetables with sugar and vinegar in a kettle. Tie spices in a cheesecloth bag; add to vegetable mixture and boil 30 minutes (start timing when mixture bubbles). Pack hot relish into hot jars, leaving ¼-inch headspace. Adjust caps.

Process pints 10 minutes in a boiling water bath canner.

Yield: about 8 pints

NOTE: You can substitute your favorite vegetables, such as green tomatoes and cabbage, for the ingredients listed.

*Vicki Shook, Wichita, Kansas
(Kansas State Fair, Hutchinson, Kansas)*

Green Tomato Relish

1 quart chopped green tomatoes
1 large sweet white onion,
  chopped
1 large sweet red pepper, chopped
2 tablespoons salt
1 cup sugar
1 tablespoon prepared mustard
1 teaspoon celery salt
4 whole cloves
1 cup vinegar, 5% acidity

Combine tomatoes, onion, and pepper in a large bowl. Sprinkle salt over vegetables and let stand 1 hour.

Prepare home canning jars and lids according to manufacturer's instructions.

Drain vegetables. Combine drained vegetables, sugar, mustard, and celery salt in a large cooking pot. Tie cloves in a cheesecloth bag and add to mixture. Stir in vinegar and simmer 20 minutes. Discard spice bag. Pack hot relish into hot jars, leaving ¼-inch headspace. Adjust caps.

Process half-pints 10 minutes in a boiling water bath canner.

Yield: about 5 half-pints

NOTE: I use this relish in potato salad and in chicken and tuna salads.

Crystal B. Stewart, Ruston, Louisiana (Ag Expo 1990, Monroe, Louisiana)

Tuna Salad

1 (6½ ounce) can white chunk tuna,
  drained
½ cup canned sweet green peas, drained
½ cup finely chopped celery
¼ cup Green Tomato Relish
¼ cup grated sweet white onion
2 hard-boiled eggs, grated
¼ cup mayonnaise
1 tablespoon sugar
Lettuce leaves (for serving plates)

Place tuna in a large bowl and flake. Add all remaining ingredients and toss lightly. Serve on lettuce leaves.

Yield: 4 servings

Crystal B. Stewart, Ruston, Louisiana (Ag Expo 1990, Monroe, Louisiana)

Green Tomato Pickle Relish

4 quarts sliced green tomatoes
3 sweet green peppers, chopped
3 stalks celery, chopped
6 onions, chopped
2 cups sugar
1 tablespoon whole cloves
1 tablespoon allspice
1 tablespoon mustard seed
2 teaspoons salt
1 quart cider vinegar, 5% acidity

Prepare home canning jars and lids according to manufacturer's instructions.

Combine all ingredients in a large saucepan; simmer 45 minutes. Pack hot relish into hot jars, leaving ¼-inch headspace. Adjust caps.

Process pints 10 minutes in a boiling water bath canner.

Yield: about 14 pints

NOTE: This relish is delicious served with roast beef, baked chicken, or pork chops.

Terry Swann, Selbyville, Delaware (Maryland State Fair, Timonium, Maryland)

Hot Relish

8 quarts chopped green tomatoes
4 quarts chopped onions
4 quarts chopped sweet green
  peppers
4 quarts hot peppers, chopped
  (include a few red peppers)
½ cup salt
8 cups sugar
4 tablespoons mustard seed
3 tablespoons turmeric
1 tablespoon celery seed
5 cups vinegar, 5% acidity

Combine all vegetables in a large bowl; add salt and let stand overnight.

Prepare home canning jars and lids according to manufacturer's instructions.

Rinse and drain vegetables. Combine sugar, spices, and vinegar in a large saucepan; bring to a boil. Add drained vegetables and simmer 10 minutes. Pack hot relish into hot jars, leaving ¼-inch headspace. Adjust caps.

Process pints 10 minutes in a boiling water bath canner.

Yield: about 25 pints

NOTE: This relish is delicious served with vegetables and meats. When cutting or seeding hot peppers, wear rubber gloves to prevent burning of hands.

Lois Tingle, Montevallo, Alabama
(Alabama State Fair,
Birmingham, Alabama)

Granny's Relish

2 cups chopped green tomatoes
2 cups chopped cabbage
2 cups chopped sweet red pepper
2 cups chopped sweet green
  pepper
2 cups chopped onion
½ cup salt
3½ cups sugar
1 teaspoon celery seed
1 teaspoon mustard seed
¾ teaspoon turmeric
2 cups cider vinegar, 5% acidity
1 cup water

Combine all vegetables in a colander to drain. Place drained vegetables in a large bowl. Sprinkle salt over vegetables and let stand 4 hours.

Prepare home canning jars and lids according to manufacturer's instructions.

Rinse vegetables well with cold water, then drain; rinse and drain again. (If vegetables are too salty, rinse and drain a third time.) Press out excess liquid. Combine sugar, spices, vinegar, and water in a large saucepan; bring to a boil. Add drained vegetables and return to a boil. Pack hot relish into hot jars, leaving ¼-inch headspace. Adjust caps.

Process pints 10 minutes in a boiling water bath canner.

Yield: about 7 pints

NOTE: I give jars of this relish as gifts at Christmas.

Alice Like, Murray, Kentucky
(Murray-Calloway County Fair, Murray, Kentucky)

Sweet Relish

3 cups chopped sweet onions
10 cups chopped yellow squash
  (remove seeds if they are too
  big)
10 cups chopped cucumbers
  (remove seeds if they are too
  big)
1 large sweet green pepper,
  chopped
1 (4 ounce) jar chopped
  pimientos
¼ cup salt
1½ teaspoons turmeric
5¾ cups sugar
2 teaspoons celery seed
2 teaspoons mustard seed
½ teaspoon mace
3 cups cider vinegar, 5% acidity

Combine all prepared vegetables and pimientos with salt and turmeric; mix well. Let stand about 2 hours.

Prepare home canning jars and lids according to manufacturer's instructions.

Drain vegetables. Combine sugar, celery seed, mustard seed, mace, and vinegar in a large saucepan; bring to a boil, stirring frequently. Add well-drained vegetables and return to a boil. Pack hot relish into hot jars, leaving ¼-inch headspace. Adjust caps.

Process pints 10 minutes in a boiling water bath canner.

Yield: about 11 pints

NOTE: This relish goes well with dried beans and with hot dogs. Use it in any recipe that calls for pickle relish.

Wanda Davis, New Hope, Kentucky (Nelson County Fair, Bardstown, Kentucky)

Pickled Cheese Ball

4 (5 ounce) packages corned beef
4 green onions (bottoms only)
2 (8 ounce) packages cream cheese,
  softened
¼ cup Sweet Relish
1 tablespoon Worcestershire sauce
Chopped pecans or walnuts (optional)

Chop corned beef and onions into small pieces. Combine all ingredients except nuts in a bowl; mix well. Form mixture into a ball. Roll ball in nuts, if desired. Refrigerate overnight.

Yield: 3 cups

Ball Recipe

Zucchini Relish

10 cups grated zucchini
4 onions, chopped
3 tablespoons salt
2 sweet red peppers, grated
2 sweet green peppers, grated
4 cups sugar
1 teaspoon cornstarch
1 teaspoon nutmeg
1 teaspoon turmeric
1 teaspoon dry mustard
1 teaspoon celery seed
2¼ cups vinegar, 5% acidity

In a large crock or container, combine zucchini, onions, and salt; mix well. Let stand overnight.

Prepare home canning jars and lids according to manufacturer's instructions.

Drain zucchini and onions. Combine drained vegetables with all remaining ingredients in a large cooking pot; bring to a boil. Boil 30 minutes, stirring occasionally. Pack hot relish into hot jars, leaving ¼-inch headspace. Adjust caps.

Process pints 10 minutes in a boiling water bath canner.

Yield: about 5 pints

*Victoria Mowrey, Tampa, Florida
(Florida State Fair, Tampa,
Florida)*

Vicki's Macaroni Salad

1 (8 ounce) package elbow macaroni,
  cooked according to package directions
¾ cup Zucchini Relish
¼ cup minced onion
6 ounces feta cheese, crumbled
2 hard-boiled eggs, diced
½ cup salad dressing
1½ tablespoons horseradish
1 tablespoon prepared mustard
1 teaspoon tarragon
1 teaspoon celery salt
½ teaspoon dry mustard
Salt and pepper to taste

Combine all ingredients in a bowl; mix
well. Refrigerate overnight.

Yield: 8 servings

NOTE: Feta cheese is salty, so be careful
not to oversalt the salad.

*Victoria Mowrey, Tampa, Florida (Florida
State Fair, Tampa, Florida)*

Bean Medley

1 quart canned red beans, drained
½ cup Squash Relish
½ cup chopped celery

Combine all ingredients in a bowl; mix
well. Cover and refrigerate 6 hours or
overnight to allow flavors to blend.

Yield: 10 to 12 servings

*Dana Kerby, Canyon, Texas (Amarillo Tri-
State Fair, Amarillo, Texas)*

Squash Relish

12 cups grated or chopped yellow
   squash
4 cups chopped onions
2 large sweet green peppers,
   chopped
1 or 2 chilies, chopped (optional)
1 (4 ounce) jar chopped
   pimientos, drained
5 tablespoons salt
5 cups sugar
2 teaspoons mixed pickling spice
1 teaspoon turmeric
1 teaspoon celery seed
2½ cups vinegar, 5% acidity

Combine vegetables and salt in a large kettle; mix well. Cover and let stand overnight.

Prepare home canning jars and lids according to manufacturer's instructions.

Drain vegetables; rinse with cold water and drain again. Return drained vegetables to large kettle. Combine sugar, spices, and vinegar in a saucepan; boil 5 minutes or until sugar dissolves. Pour hot liquid over vegetables and boil 5 minutes. Pack hot relish into hot jars, leaving ¼-inch headspace. Adjust caps.

Process pints 10 minutes in a boiling water bath canner.

Yield: about 6 pints

NOTE: This is a very colorful relish to serve with black-eyed peas or red pinto beans. When cutting or seeding hot peppers, wear rubber gloves to prevent burning of hands.

Dana Kerby, Canyon, Texas (Amarillo Tri-State Fair, Amarillo, Texas)

Winter Salad Relish

2 quarts mixed yellow and green
  squash slices
1 quart cauliflowerets
1 quart small carrot slices
1 quart onion rings
1 quart tiny whole okra pods
1 quart mixed sweet red and green
  pepper rings
3 quarts water
1 quart vinegar, 5% acidity
1 cup salt

Prepare home canning jars and
lids according to manufacturer's
instructions.

Wash and prepare all vegetables.
Mix vegetables and pack into hot
jars, leaving ¼-inch headspace.
Combine water, vinegar, and salt
in a saucepan; bring to a boil.
Pour hot liquid over vegetables,
leaving ¼-inch headspace.
Remove air bubbles with a non-
metallic spatula. Adjust caps.

Process pints 15 minutes in a
boiling water bath canner.

Yield: about 14 pints

NOTE: Use freshly picked
vegetables for best results.

*Edna Alexander, Harrison,
Arkansas (Northwest Arkansas
District Fair, Harrison, Arkansas)*

Spicy Salsa

5 pounds tomatoes, peeled, cored
  and chopped
1 pound sweet green peppers,
  chopped
1 pound jalapeño peppers, seeded
  and chopped
1 pound onions, chopped
1 cup cider vinegar, 5% acidity
2 cloves garlic, minced
3 teaspoons salt
½ teaspoon pepper

Prepare home canning jars and
lids according to manufacturer's
instructions.

Combine all ingredients in a large
saucepot and bring to a boil.
Reduce heat and simmer about 20
minutes. Pour hot salsa into hot
jars, leaving ¼-inch headspace.

Process pints 15 minutes in a
boiling water bath canner.

Yield: about 7 pints

NOTE: When cutting or seeding
hot peppers, wear rubber gloves to
prevent burning of hands.

Ball Recipe

Sweet Onion Relish with a Bite

2 large Bermuda onions, peeled and diced
2 tablespoons butter or margarine
1 tablespoon water
7 tablespoons sugar
2 cups Spicy Salsa

Sauté onions in butter or margarine until they are whitish-pink in color; do not brown. Add water to help keep the onions from browning. Sprinkle sugar over onions, 2 tablespoons at a time, and simmer. Stir in salsa and simmer until mixture is reduced to desired consistency.

Serve warm or at room temperature, with chips or cheese and crackers.

Yield: about 2 cups

NOTE: Use more or less sugar, depending on the amount of onion—the flavor should be sugary first, then the onion flavor takes over. For less bite, use medium or mild salsa. Excellent as a hot dog relish.

Scott D. O'Brien, Indianapolis, Indiana
(Indiana State Fair, Indianapolis, Indiana)

JELLIES & SEMI-SOFT SPREADS

APPLE BUTTER 134 ▪ CARAMEL SPICE APPLE BUTTER 135 ▪ Apple
Butter Bread 136 ▪ MAPLE APPLE JAM 137 ▪ Maple Apple Tea Ring 138 ▪
APPLE CINNAMON JELLY 139 ▪ Thumbprint Cookies 140 ▪ RED HOT
APPLE JELLY 141 ▪ APPLE PRESERVES 142 ▪ Apple Preserves Coffee
Cake 143 ▪ APRICOT PINEAPPLE JAM 144 ▪ Apricot-Pineapple Banana Nut
Bread 145 ▪ BLACKBERRY JAM 146 ▪ Jam Cake 147 ▪ Peek-a-Jam Muffins 148
▪ BLUEBERRY SPICE JAM 149 ▪ Jam-Filled Cookies 150 ▪ BUFFALO
BERRY JELLY 151 ▪ CHAMPAGNE JELLY 152 ▪ FIG PRESERVES 153 ▪ Fig
Cake 154 ▪ FRESH FIG CONSERVE 155 ▪ FRESH GRAPEFRUIT WINE
JELLY 156 ▪ ORANGE LEMON MARMALADE 157 ▪ Lemonade Coffee
Cake 158 ▪ PEACH PRESERVES 159 ▪ Dessert Fruit Tarts 160 ▪ Peach Cookie
Squares 161 ▪ PEAR JAM 162, 164 ▪ Toasted Pear Triangles 163 ▪ PEAR
JELLY 165 ▪ Jelly-Filled Oat Muffins 166 ▪ PLUM JELLY 167 ▪ RASPBERRY
JAM 168 ▪ Jam-Filled Lattice-Top Coffee Cake 169 ▪ RHUBARB JELLY 170 ▪
Jelly Muffins 171 ▪ RHUBARB RASPBERRY JAM 172 ▪ The Big Cookie 173 ▪
RHUBARB PEACH JAM 174 ▪ Jam Good Roll 175 ▪ SERVICEBERRY
JELLY 176 ▪ STRAWBERRY PRESERVES 177 ▪ Strawberry Coffee Cake 178 ▪
STRAWBERRY RHUBARB JAM 179 ▪ Blushing Angel 179 ▪ Tomato
Marmalade 180

JELLIES & SEMI-SOFT SPREADS

Apple Butter

2¼ quarts sugarless smooth
  applesauce (about 7 pounds
  apples)
4 cups sugar
1 teaspoon cinnamon
½ teaspoon cloves
½ cup vinegar
½ cup water

Combine all ingredients in a large kettle to cook on top of the stove, or in a 9 × 13-inch pan to cook in the oven (at 300°F). Cook mixture approximately 3 hours, stirring every 15 minutes. When apple butter will come to a peak and stay, it is ready to put in jars.

Prepare home canning jars and lids according to manufacturer's instructions.

Pour hot apple butter into hot jars, leaving ¼-inch headspace. Adjust caps.

Process half-pints 10 minutes in a boiling water bath canner.

Yield: about 7 half-pints

NOTE: This makes a deep brown butter that spreads on toast very easily. I increase this recipe by five times and cook it in my large electric roasting pan, uncovered, at 350°F for 12 to 14 hours, stirring frequently.

Charlene Daniels, Groton, New York (New York State Fair, Syracuse, New York)

Caramel Spice Apple Butter

9 to 10 Rome apples
9 to 10 Granny Smith apples
1 cup water
4 cups sugar, divided
1 teaspoon cinnamon
½ teaspoon cloves
¼ teaspoon ginger
2 tablespoons lemon juice

Prepare home canning jars and lids according to manufacturer's instructions.

Wash and quarter apples. Combine apples and water in a large saucepot; cover and cook until soft (about 30 minutes). Press apples through a food mill. Measure 12 cups apple pulp into saucepot. Heat 2 cups sugar in a three-quart saucepan, stirring until sugar melts and turns a rich golden brown. Carefully pour melted sugar into apple pulp (sugar will crackle and harden); add remaining 2 cups sugar and spices. Cook, uncovered, about 1 hour or until apple butter thickens, stirring occasionally to prevent sticking. Stir in lemon juice. Pour hot apple butter into hot jars, leaving ¼-inch headspace. Adjust caps.

Process half-pints 10 minutes in a boiling water bath canner.

Yield: about 5 half-pints

Ball Recipe

Apple Butter Bread

2 cups all-purpose flour
1 cup brown sugar
1½ teaspoons baking powder
½ teaspoon baking soda
½ teaspoon salt
¾ pint (1½ cups) Caramel Spice Apple
   Butter, divided
½ cup apple juice
¼ cup (½ stick) butter or margarine,
   melted
1 egg, beaten
1 cup raisins
½ cup chopped walnuts

Preheat oven to 350°F. Grease and flour bottom and sides of a 9x5x2¾-inch loaf pan; set aside.

Combine flour, brown sugar, baking powder, soda, and salt in a large bowl. Stir in ¾ cup apple butter, apple juice, butter or margarine, and egg. Fold in raisins and walnuts. Pour half of the batter into prepared pan. Spread remaining ¾ cup apple butter over batter. Gently pour remaining batter over apple butter.

Bake at 350°F for 65 to 75 minutes or until top springs back when lightly touched in center. Set pan on a wire rack to cool for 15 minutes, then remove bread from pan and continue cooling on rack. Wrap bread tightly with plastic wrap and store in refrigerator.

Yield: 1 loaf

Ball Recipe

Maple Apple Jam

2 quarts finely chopped peeled
  apples (about 6 pounds apples)
1 cup apple cider
¾ cup pure maple syrup
1 tablespoon lemon juice
½ teaspoon cinnamon

Prepare home canning jars and lids according to manufacturer's instructions.

Combine all ingredients in a large kettle and bring to a boil; boil until mixture thickens (about 10 minutes). Jam is ready when it begins to hold its shape when dropped onto a cold plate. Remove from heat; skim off any foam. Pour hot jam into hot jars, leaving ¼-inch headspace. Adjust caps.

Process half-pints 10 minutes in a boiling water bath canner.

Yield: about 6 half-pints

NOTE: This jam tastes just like apple pie in a jar.

Cindy Tufts, Carmichael, California (California State Fair, Sacramento, California)

Maple Apple Tea Ring

5¼ cups all-purpose flour, divided
2 packages dry yeast
½ cup sugar
1 teaspoon salt
1 cup milk
½ cup water
¼ cup (½ stick) butter or margarine
2 eggs
½ to ¾ cup Maple Apple Jam, divided
½ cup chopped walnuts, divided
Confectioners' sugar glaze (optional)

Preheat oven to 350°F.

Combine 2½ cups flour, yeast, sugar, and salt in a large mixing bowl; mix well. Heat milk, water, and butter or margarine until warm (120°F to 130°F); butter does not need to melt. Add hot liquid to flour mixture. Add eggs. Blend at low speed of electric mixer until moistened, then beat 3 minutes at medium speed. By hand, gradually stir in enough remaining flour to make a soft dough. Knead dough on a floured surface until smooth and elastic (about 5 to 8 minutes). Place dough in a greased bowl, turning to grease top. Cover and let rise in a warm place about 1 hour or until doubled in bulk.

Punch dough down and divide into two portions. On a lightly floured surface, roll each portion of dough into a 15x12-inch rectangle. Spread half of the jam on each rectangle of dough; sprinkle nuts over jam. Starting at long side of rectangle, tightly roll up each portion of dough; pinch edges to seal. Form rolls into rings; pinch ends to seal. Place each ring seam side down on a greased cookie sheet. With scissors, make cuts one inch apart through tops of rings, leaving bottom of ring intact. Pull out each slice, turning it on its side. Cover rings and let rise in a warm place about 20 minutes or until almost doubled in bulk.

Bake rings at 350°F for 20 to 25 minutes or until golden brown. Remove from cookie sheets to cool. Drizzle with confectioners' sugar glaze, if desired.

Yield: 10 to 12 servings

*Cindy Tufts, Carmichael, California
(California State Fair, Sacramento, California)*

Apple Cinnamon Jelly

5 pounds Golden Delicious
  apples
5 cups water
10 cinnamon sticks
Red food coloring
1 package powdered pectin
9 cups sugar

Wash apples. Remove blossom and stem ends from apples, then cut into chunks. Combine apples and water in a large saucepot; cover and simmer 10 minutes, stirring occasionally. Crush apples; simmer 5 minutes longer. Place prepared apples in a dampened jelly bag and let juice drip for several hours.

Prepare home canning jars and lids according to manufacturer's instructions. Jars should be covered with water and boiled 10 to 15 minutes to sterilize.

Measure 7 cups apple juice into an eight-quart saucepot; bring to a boil. Remove from heat and add cinnamon sticks; cover and let steep 20 minutes. Discard cinnamon sticks. Add a few drops of food coloring to give juice a nice pink color; add pectin. Bring to a full, rolling boil over high heat, stirring constantly. Add sugar and return to a full, rolling boil. Boil hard 1 minute, stirring constantly. Remove from heat; skim off foam. Pour hot jelly into hot jars, leaving ¼-inch headspace. Adjust caps.

Process half-pints 5 minutes in a boiling water bath canner.

Yield: about 10 half-pints

Julie Speck, Auburn, New York (New York State Fair, Syracuse, New York)

Thumbprint Cookies

¼ cup (½ stick) margarine, softened
¼ cup shortening
¼ cup packed brown sugar
1 egg, separated
½ teaspoon vanilla
1 cup all-purpose flour
¼ teaspoon salt
¾ cup finely chopped walnuts
1 cup Apple Cinnamon Jelly

Preheat oven to 350°F.

Combine margarine, shortening, brown sugar, egg yolk, and vanilla; mix until well blended. Work in flour and salt until dough holds together. Shape dough by teaspoonfuls into one-inch balls. Beat egg white slightly. Dip each ball into egg white, then roll in nuts. Place balls one inch apart on ungreased baking sheet. Using your thumb, press deeply into center of each ball.

Bake at 350°F about 10 minutes or until lightly browned. Remove from baking sheet immediately to cool. Fill each thumbprint with a spoonful of jelly.

Yield: 3 dozen cookies

Julie Speck, Auburn, New York (New York State Fair, Syracuse, New York)

Red Hot Apple Jelly

5 pounds medium-ripe golden
  apples
5 cups water
½ cup lemon juice
1 (¾ ounce) box red hot
  cinnamon candies
1 package powdered pectin
1 teaspoon butter or margarine
6 cups sugar

Sort and wash apples; remove stems and leaves but do not peel or core. Cut apples into small pieces. Combine apples and water in an eight-quart kettle; bring to a boil over high heat. Reduce heat and simmer 20 to 25 minutes or until fruit is soft. Extract juice.

Prepare home canning jars and lids according to manufacturer's instructions. Jars should be covered with water and boiled 10 to 15 minutes to sterilize.

Measure 5 cups apple juice into an eight-quart kettle. Add lemon juice, cinnamon candies, pectin, and butter or margarine, stirring well; bring to a boil over high heat. Add sugar when juice starts to boil; return to a boil, stirring constantly. Boil hard 2 minutes. Remove from heat; skim off foam, if necessary. Pour hot jelly into hot jars, leaving ¼-inch headspace. Adjust caps.

Process half-pints 5 minutes in a boiling water bath canner.

Yield: about 9 half-pints

Russ Firestone Family, Selah, Washington (Central Washington State Fair, Yakima, Washington)

Apple Preserves

6 cups peeled, cored and sliced
   apples
1 cup water
1 tablespoon lemon juice
1 package powdered pectin
½ cup thin lemon slices (about 1
   medium lemon)
4 cups sugar
2 teaspoons nutmeg

Prepare home canning jars and lids according to manufacturer's instructions.

Combine apples, water, and lemon juice in a large saucepot; cover and simmer 10 minutes. Stir in pectin and bring to a rolling boil, stirring frequently. Add lemon slices and sugar, stirring to dissolve sugar; return to a rolling boil. Boil hard 1 minute, stirring frequently. Remove from heat. Add nutmeg. Skim off foam, if necessary. Pour hot preserves into hot jars, leaving ¼-inch headspace. Adjust caps.

Process half-pints 10 minutes in a boiling water bath canner.

Yield: about 6 half-pints

Ball Recipe

Apple Preserves Coffee Cake

CAKE

2½ cups all-purpose flour
1 cup sugar
1 cup (2 sticks) butter or margarine
½ teaspoon baking powder
½ teaspoon baking soda
¼ teaspoon salt
¾ cup dairy sour cream
2 teaspoons vanilla
1 egg

FILLING

1 (8 ounce) package cream cheese,
  softened
½ cup confectioners' sugar
1 egg
1 teaspoon lemon juice
2 teaspoons grated lemon rind
1½ cups Apple Preserves

TOPPING

1 cup reserved crumb mixture (from cake)
2 teaspoons grated lemon rind

Preheat oven to 350°F. Grease and flour bottom and sides of a nine- or ten-inch springform pan; set aside.

To make Cake: Combine flour and sugar; using a pastry blender or fork, cut in butter or margarine until mixture resembles coarse crumbs. Reserve 1 cup crumb mixture for topping. To remaining crumb mixture, add baking powder, soda, salt, sour cream, vanilla, and egg; blend well. Spread batter evenly in prepared pan.

To make Filling: In a small bowl, combine cream cheese, confectioners' sugar, egg, lemon juice, and lemon rind; blend well. Pour filling over cake batter in pan. Carefully spoon preserves over cream cheese mixture.

To make Topping: In a small bowl, combine reserved crumb mixture and lemon rind. Sprinkle over preserves.

Bake at 350°F for 45 to 55 minutes or until cream cheese filling is set and crust is golden brown. Cool 15 minutes on a wire rack before removing sides of pan. Refrigerate any leftovers.

Yield: 16 servings

Ball Recipe

Apricot Pineapple Jam

3½ cups chopped fresh apricots
  (about 1½ pounds apricots)
1½ cups drained unsweetened
  crushed pineapple (about 1
  pound pineapple)
¼ cup lemon juice
1 package powdered pectin
7 cups sugar

Prepare home canning jars and lids according to manufacturer's instructions.

Combine apricots, pineapple, lemon juice, and pectin in a six- or eight-quart saucepan; bring to a boil. Add sugar and return to a boil. Boil hard 1 minute. Pour hot jam into hot jars, leaving ¼-inch headspace. Adjust caps.

Process half-pints 10 minutes in a boiling water bath canner.

Yield: about 8 half-pints

Lynn Matranga, Ontario, California (Los Angeles County Fair, Pomona, California)

Apricot-Pineapple Banana Nut Bread

1 cup Apricot Pineapple Jam, divided
2½ cups flour
1 cup sugar
1 cup chopped nuts
3½ teaspoons baking powder
1 teaspoon salt
1 cup mashed banana
¾ cup milk
1 egg
3 tablespoons vegetable oil

Preheat oven to 325°F. Grease and flour a 9x5x3-inch baking pan; set aside.

Combine half of the jam with all remaining ingredients in a large bowl; mix well (1 minute with electric mixer or 50 strokes by hand). Pour batter into prepared pan.

Bake at 325°F for approximately 1 hour or until toothpick inserted in center comes out clean. Cool 20 minutes. Remove from pan and place on serving plate. Spoon remaining jam over bread.

Yield: 6 to 8 servings

NOTE: Always place pan in top center of oven and turn pan halfway through baking.

Lynn Matranga, Ontario, California (Los Angeles County Fair, Pomona, California)

Blackberry Jam

2¼ quarts blackberries, crushed
   (about 4 pounds blackberries)
6 cups sugar

Prepare home canning jars and lids according to manufacturer's instructions.

Combine crushed berries and sugar in a large saucepan; bring to a boil slowly, stirring until sugar dissolves. Cook rapidly to jellying point (8°F above the boiling point of water). As mixture thickens, stir frequently to prevent sticking. Pour hot jam into hot jars, leaving ¼-inch headspace. Adjust caps.

Process pints 15 minutes in a boiling water bath canner.

Yield: about 3 pints

Beulah Devine, Sacramento, Kentucky (McLean County Fair, Calhoun, Kentucky)

Jam Cake

CAKE

3 cups sifted all-purpose flour
1 teaspoon cinnamon
1 teaspoon nutmeg
1 teaspoon allspice
1 teaspoon cloves
2 cups sugar
½ pound (2 sticks) butter or margarine
5 large eggs, well beaten
1 teaspoon baking soda
1 cup buttermilk
1½ pints (3 cups) Blackberry Jam
1 (8 ounce) can crushed pineapple, drained
1 cup chopped pecans

ICING

1 cup packed brown sugar
½ cup (1 stick) butter or margarine
½ cup evaporated milk
2 cups confectioners' sugar
Pecan halves (for garnish)

Preheat oven to 325°F.

To make Cake: Sift flour with spices; set aside. Cream sugar and butter or margarine; add eggs. Dissolve soda in buttermilk. Add flour mixture and buttermilk to creamed mixture, a small amount at a time, beating well. Add jam, pineapple, and pecans; mix well. Spread batter in three waxed paper lined nine-inch cake pans.

Bake at 325°F for approximately 30 minutes. Cool.

To make Icing: Combine brown sugar and butter or margarine in a saucepan; heat over low heat, stirring until butter melts and mixture is bubbling. Add evaporated milk and boil 1 minute. Remove from heat; add confectioners' sugar, mixing until smooth. Spread icing lightly between layers and on top and sides of cake. Decorate top of cake with pecans, if desired.

Yield: 10 to 12 servings

NOTE: Instead of using 3 cups of blackberry jam, you can use 2 cups of blackberry jam and 1 cup of peach or strawberry preserves, if desired. I make a double batch of icing.

Beulah Devine, Sacramento, Kentucky
(McLean County Fair, Calhoun, Kentucky)

Peek-a-Jam Muffins

2 cups all-purpose flour
4 teaspoons baking powder
½ teaspoon salt
2 tablespoons sugar
1 cup milk
1 egg
3 tablespoons shortening, melted and
  cooled slightly
⅓ cup Blackberry Jam

Preheat oven to 425°F.

Combine flour, baking powder, and salt in a bowl; mix lightly. Mix in sugar; set aside. Combine milk and egg, mixing until well blended. Add shortening to milk mixture. Combine dry ingredients with milk mixture, mixing enough to moisten all ingredients. Spoon just enough batter into well-greased muffin cups to cover bottom of cups. Spoon 1 teaspoon of jam into the center of the batter in each muffin cup. Add enough additional batter to each cup to fill two-thirds full.

Bake at 425°F for 10 to 15 minutes.

Yield: 15 muffins

Paula Faught, New Haven, Kentucky
(Nelson County Fair, Bardstown, Kentucky)

Blueberry Spice Jam

2½ pints ripe blueberries (about
    2½ pounds blueberries)
¾ cup water
1 tablespoon lemon juice
½ teaspoon cinnamon
1 package powdered pectin
5½ cups sugar

Wash blueberries. Thoroughly crush berries, one layer at a time, in a saucepan. Add water, lemon juice, and cinnamon; stir in pectin. Bring to a full, rolling boil over high heat, stirring frequently. Add sugar and return to a full, rolling boil. Boil hard 1 minute, stirring constantly. Remove from heat; skim off foam. Pour hot jam into hot jars, leaving ¼-inch headspace. Adjust caps.

Process half-pints 15 minutes in a boiling water bath canner.

Yield: about 5 half-pints

Deidra Johnson, Riverton, Wyoming (Wyoming State Fair, Douglas, Wyoming)

Jam-Filled Cookies

2 cups sifted flour
¼ teaspoon salt
1 cup (2 sticks) margarine
½ cup packed brown sugar
2 egg yolks
½ teaspoon vanilla
1 cup finely chopped pecans
½ cup Blueberry Spice Jam

Preheat oven to 350°F.

Sift together flour and salt; set aside. Combine margarine and brown sugar in a mixing bowl; cream at medium speed of electric mixer until light and fluffy. Add egg yolks and vanilla, beating well. Gradually stir dry ingredients into creamed mixture, blending well. Shape dough into one-inch balls. Roll balls in pecans and place about two inches apart on ungreased baking sheets.

Bake at 350°F for 5 minutes. Remove from oven and, with your finger, make a depression in the center of each cookie. Return cookies to oven and bake 8 minutes longer. Remove cookies from baking sheets and cool on racks. When cookies are completely cooled, fill depression in each with ½ teaspoon jam.

Yield: 3½ dozen cookies

*Deidra Johnson, Riverton, Wyoming
(Wyoming State Fair, Douglas, Wyoming)*

Buffalo Berry Jelly

1 quart buffalo berries
3 cups water
1 package powdered pectin
7 cups sugar

Combine berries and water in a saucepan; boil gently until berries are tender (15 to 20 minutes). Extract juice by straining berries through a jelly bag. Squeeze bag; strain again.

Prepare home canning jars and lids according to manufacturer's instructions. Jars should be covered with water and boiled 10 to 15 minutes to sterilize.

Measure 5 cups buffalo berry juice. (If there is not enough juice to make 5 cups, add water, apple juice, or crab apple juice to make up the difference.) Combine juice and pectin in a six-quart kettle; bring to a boil. Stir in sugar and boil rapidly until jelling point is reached (about 1 minute). Remove from heat; skim off foam. Pour hot jelly into hot jars, leaving ¼-inch headspace. Adjust caps.

Process half-pints 5 minutes in a boiling water bath canner.

Yield: about 10 half-pints

NOTE: Buffalo berries are tiny (about ⅛ inch in diameter), orange-red in color, and they have a very distinctive tart flavor.

Mildred E. Meyer, Billings, Montana (MontanaFair, Billings, Montana)

Champagne Jelly

1 (750 ml) bottle champagne
1 package powdered pectin
4 cups sugar

Prepare home canning jars and lids according to manufacturer's instructions. Jars should be covered with water and boiled 10 to 15 minutes to sterilize.

Combine champagne and pectin in a large cooking pot; bring to a boil, stirring constantly. Stir in sugar and boil hard 2 minutes. Remove from heat; skim off foam. Pour hot jelly into hot jars, leaving ¼-inch headspace. Adjust caps.

Process half-pints 5 minutes in a boiling water bath canner.

Yield: about 5 half-pints

NOTE: If you use clear champagne, you can add a drop of red food coloring to make the jelly pink, if you wish.

Clarissa Tuor, Santa Rosa, California (Sonoma County Fair, Santa Rosa, California)

Fig Preserves

2 quarts firm, ripe figs, peeled
  (about 5 pounds figs)
1 medium lemon, sliced
6 cups sugar
2 cups water

Combine figs and lemon slices. Combine sugar and water in a large, heavy pot; bring to a boil, stirring frequently until sugar dissolves. Add fruit to syrup; reduce heat and boil gently, uncovered, 1 to 1½ hours or until figs are clear and syrup is the consistency of honey. Shake pot occasionally while cooking but do not stir. Remove pot from heat, cover, and let stand in a cool place overnight. (This will make the figs plump.)

Prepare home canning jars and lids according to manufacturer's instructions.

Bring fig mixture to a boil. Remove from heat; skim off foam, if necessary. Pour hot preserves into hot jars, leaving ¼-inch headspace. Adjust caps.

Process pints 15 minutes in a boiling water bath canner.

Yield: about 5 pints

NOTE: If you prefer unpeeled figs, they do just as well.

Dorothy Glover, Coushatta, Louisiana (Red River Parish Fair, Coushatta, Louisiana)

Fig Cake

2 cups all-purpose flour
1 teaspoon cinnamon
1 teaspoon nutmeg
1 teaspoon allspice
1 teaspoon salt
3 eggs
1½ cups sugar
1 cup vegetable oil
1 teaspoon baking soda
2 teaspoons hot water
½ cup buttermilk
1 cup chopped Fig Preserves with juice
1 cup chopped pecans
1 teaspoon vanilla extract

Preheat oven to 350°F.

Sift together flour, spices, and salt; set aside. In a three-quart mixing bowl, beat eggs with electric mixer until thick and lemon colored. Add sugar and oil; beat well. Dissolve soda in hot water; combine with buttermilk. Add dry ingredients alternately with buttermilk to creamed mixture, mixing well. Stir in preserves, pecans, and vanilla. Pour batter into a greased and floured ten-inch tube pan.

Bake at 350°F for 1 hour and 10 to 15 minutes. Cool 20 to 30 minutes before removing from pan.

Yield: 12 to 16 servings

NOTE: This cake is delicious and a good "keeper." It also freezes well.

Dorothy Glover, Coushatta, Louisiana (Red River Parish Fair, Coushatta, Louisiana)

Fresh Fig Conserve

1 quart fresh figs (about 2½
  pounds figs)
2½ cups sugar
⅓ cup lemon juice
1 tablespoon grated orange peel
¼ cup chopped walnuts

Rinse figs. Clip and discard stems, then chop figs. Combine 3 cups chopped figs and sugar in a five-quart pot, stirring until well blended; let stand 1 hour.

Prepare home canning jars and lids according to manufacturer's instructions.

Bring figs and sugar to a boil over medium heat; cook, uncovered and stirring often, about 20 minutes or until thickened. Stir in lemon juice, orange peel, and walnuts; return to a boil. Boil hard 3 minutes, stirring often. Pour hot conserve into hot jars, leaving ¼-inch headspace. Adjust caps.

Process half-pints 15 minutes in a boiling water bath canner.

Yield: about 5 half-pints

NOTE: Delicious on toast, french toast, or baking powder biscuits.

Warren L. Knudtson, Las Vegas, Nevada (Las Vegas Jaycees State Fair, Las Vegas, Nevada)

Fresh Grapefruit Wine Jelly

1 cup freshly squeezed grapefruit
   juice, strained
1 cup ruby red Port wine (or
   claret or sauterne wine)
1 cup water
1 package powdered pectin
3¾ cups sugar

Prepare home canning jars and lids according to manufacturer's instructions. Jars should be covered with water and boiled 10 to 15 minutes to sterilize.

Combine grapefruit juice, wine, water, and pectin in a heavy saucepan; stir until pectin dissolves. Bring to a full, rolling boil over high heat, stirring constantly. Add sugar all at once and return to a boil. Boil hard 2 minutes, stirring constantly. Remove from heat; skim off foam, if necessary. Pour hot jelly into hot jars, leaving ¼-inch headspace. Adjust caps.

Process half-pints 10 minutes in a boiling water bath canner.

Yield: about 5 half-pints

Helen H. Kirsch, Albuquerque, New Mexico (New Mexico State Fair, Albuquerque, New Mexico)

Orange Lemon Marmalade

3½ cups chopped orange pulp
   (about 4 large oranges)
3 cups thinly sliced orange peel
   (about 4 large oranges)
4 large lemons, thinly sliced
1½ quarts water
Sugar (about 5½ cups)

Combine orange pulp, peel, lemon slices, and water in a large saucepot; simmer 5 minutes. Remove pot from heat; cover and let stand 12 to 18 hours in a cool place.

Prepare home canning jars and lids according to manufacturer's instructions.

Cook fruit mixture rapidly until peel is tender (about 45 minutes). Measure fruit and liquid. Add 1 cup sugar for each cup of fruit. Bring mixture slowly to a boil, stirring until sugar dissolves. Cook rapidly to jellying point (8°F above the boiling point of water). As mixture thickens, stir frequently to prevent sticking. Pour hot marmalade into hot jars, leaving ¼-inch headspace. Adjust caps.

Process half-pints 10 minutes in a boiling water bath canner.

Yield: about 6 half-pints

Ball Recipe

Lemonade Coffee Cake

TOPPING

1 cup Orange Lemon Marmalade
1 tablespoon cornstarch
1 tablespoon margarine

CAKE

5½ cups flour, divided
2 packages yeast
1 cup sugar
1 teaspoon salt
1½ cups milk
¼ cup (½ stick) margarine
2 eggs
½ cup slivered almonds
½ teaspoon almond extract (optional)
No-stick vegetable cooking spray

Preheat oven to 350°F.

To make Topping: Combine marmalade and cornstarch in a saucepan. Add margarine and cook over low heat until thickened, stirring often; set aside.

To make Cake: Combine 2½ cups flour, yeast, sugar, and salt in a large bowl. Heat milk and margarine until warm (120°F to 130°F). Add warm liquid to dry ingredients; beat 2 minutes. Add eggs and beat 1 minute longer. By hand, stir in enough additional flour to make a soft dough. Knead dough on a floured surface until smooth and elastic (about 5 minutes). Cover and let rest 5 minutes.

Spray two nine-inch pans with no-stick cooking spray. Divide dough into two equal portions. Place one portion of dough in each pan; spread to cover bottom of pan. Spread half of the cooled topping on each piece of dough. Mix almonds with almond extract, if desired; sprinkle almonds over topping. Using a spoon, lightly press almonds and topping into dough in several places. Let rise until doubled in bulk (about 30 minutes).

Bake at 350°F for 20 to 25 minutes. If tops brown too quickly, reduce oven temperature or cover pans loosely with foil. Remove from pans and cool on racks.

Yield: 2 coffee cakes

NOTE: These coffee cakes are very light and delicious. They also freeze well.

*Maureen Luczak, Saginaw, Michigan
(Saginaw County Fair, Saginaw, Michigan)*

Peach Preserves

1 quart peeled, pitted and sliced
  peaches (about 2½ pounds
  peaches)
2 tablespoons lemon juice
1 package powdered pectin
7 cups sugar

Prepare home canning jars and lids according to manufacturer's instructions.

Combine peaches, lemon juice, and pectin in a large saucepot; bring to a rolling boil, stirring gently. Add sugar all at once and return to a boil. Boil hard 1 minute, stirring constantly. Remove from heat; skim off foam, if necessary. Pour hot preserves into hot jars, leaving ¼-inch headspace. Adjust caps.

Process half-pints 10 minutes in a boiling water bath canner.

Yield: about 9 half-pints

Louise Bodziony, Gladstone, Missouri (Ozark Empire Fair, Springfield, Missouri)

Dessert Fruit Tarts

1 (14 ounce) can sweetened condensed
  milk
2½ tablespoons lemon juice
2 ounces whipped topping
10 ounces cream cheese, softened
12 baked tart shells
¾ cup Peach Preserves

Combine sweetened condensed milk and lemon juice in a mixing bowl; beat until firm. Add whipped topping and cream cheese; mix well. Spoon filling into tart shells. Refrigerate 2 hours. Top each tart with 1 tablespoon of preserves before serving.

Yield: 12 servings

NOTE: This dessert goes well with pork entrées.

Lou Ann Stapp, Columbiana, Alabama (Alabama State Fair, Birmingham, Alabama)

Peach Cookie Squares

1½ cups all-purpose flour
½ teaspoon salt
¼ teaspoon baking soda
¼ teaspoon baking powder
1 teaspoon cinnamon
½ teaspoon allspice
½ teaspoon ginger
½ teaspoon nutmeg
¼ teaspoon cloves
½ cup (1 stick) butter or margarine,
    softened
½ cup firmly packed light brown sugar
¼ cup granulated sugar
2 extra-large eggs, at room temperature
½ cup Peach Preserves
1 tablespoon vanilla extract
1 cup chopped dried peaches
¾ cup golden raisins
¾ cup chopped pecans

Preheat oven to 350°F. Lightly butter and flour a 13x9x2-inch baking pan; set aside.

Sift flour, salt, soda, baking powder, and spices onto a sheet of waxed paper; set aside. Using an electric mixer, cream butter or margarine in a large bowl; add brown sugar and beat at medium speed of mixer 2 minutes. Add granulated sugar and beat 1 minute. Add eggs, one at a time, beating well after each addition. Blend in preserves and vanilla. Add dry ingredients, half at a time, and beat at low speed of mixer just until moistened. By hand, stir in dried peaches, raisins, and pecans. Spoon batter into prepared pan, spreading evenly with a spatula.

Place on middle rack of oven and bake at 350°F for 25 minutes or until set and firm to the touch. Cool in pan on a wire rack about 2 hours. Cut into squares to serve.

Yield: 24 squares

Louise Bodziony, Gladstone, Missouri
(Ozark Empire Fair, Springfield, Missouri)

Pear Jam

2½ pounds cooking pears
1 medium orange
1 medium lemon
¾ cup crushed pineapple,
   drained
5½ cups sugar

Prepare home canning jars and lids according to manufacturer's instructions.

Wash, peel, and core pears. Wash orange and lemon; do not peel. Grind pears, orange, and lemon, using coarse blade of food chopper. Combine ground fruit with pineapple and sugar in a saucepan; stir well. Bring to a boil and cook 20 minutes, stirring occasionally. Pour hot jam into hot jars, leaving ¼-inch headspace. Adjust caps.

Process half-pints 15 minutes in a boiling water bath canner.

Yield: about 8 half-pints

NOTE: This jam has a citrus flavor. Use as a topping on pound or white cake.

Patricia E. Jacobs, Pine Bluff, Arkansas (Southeast Arkansas District Fair, Pine Bluff, Arkansas)

Toasted Pear Triangles

---

12 slices sandwich bread
6 tablespoons cream cheese, whipped
6 tablespoons Pear Jam
Nutmeg (optional)
2 eggs
⅓ cup milk
⅛ teaspoon salt
2 tablespoons butter or margarine
Confectioners' sugar (optional)

Spread cream cheese on six slices of bread, using 1 tablespoon per slice and spreading on one side only. Spread jam over cream cheese (1 tablespoon per slice of bread); sprinkle nutmeg over jam. Top with remaining slices of bread to form "sandwiches."

Combine eggs, milk, and salt in a shallow dish; beat well. Dip each sandwich into egg mixture, turning to coat both sides.

Melt butter or margarine in a large skillet. Cook three sandwiches at a time in butter until browned, turning to brown both sides. Repeat procedure with remaining sandwiches, adding more butter to skillet if necessary.

Sprinkle browned sandwiches with confectioners' sugar. Cut each sandwich diagonally into two or four triangles. Serve immediately.

Yield: 6 servings

Ball Recipe

Pear Jam

6 pounds medium-ripe pears
¼ cup lemon juice
1 package powdered pectin
1 teaspoon butter or margarine
6 cups sugar

Prepare home canning jars and lids according to manufacturer's instructions.

Sort and wash pears. Remove stems and leaves, then peel, quarter, core, and cut pears into small pieces. Place pears in blender container and pure. Measure 4 cups pear pure into an eight-quart kettle. Add lemon juice, pectin, and butter, stirring well; bring to a boil over high heat. When mixture starts to boil, add sugar, stirring constantly. Return to a full boil and boil hard 4 minutes. Remove from heat; skim off foam, if necessary. Pour hot jam into hot jars, leaving ¼-inch headspace. Adjust caps.

Process half-pints 15 minutes in a boiling water bath canner.

Yield: about 10 half-pints

Russ Firestone Family, Selah, Washington (Central Washington State Fair, Yakima, Washington)

Pear Jelly

5 pounds medium-ripe pears
5 cups water
½ cup lemon juice
1 package powdered pectin
1 teaspoon butter or margarine
6 cups sugar

Sort and wash pears. Remove stems and leaves, but do not peel or core pears. Cut pears into small pieces. Combine cut-up pears and water in an eight-quart kettle; cover and bring to a boil over high heat. Reduce heat and simmer 20 to 25 minutes or until fruit is soft. Extract juice.

Prepare home canning jars and lids according to manufacturer's instructions. Jars should be covered with water and boiled 10 to 15 minutes to sterilize.

Measure 5 cups pear juice into an eight-quart kettle. Add lemon juice, pectin, and butter or margarine; stir well. Bring to a boil over high heat. When mixture starts to boil, add sugar, stirring constantly. Return to a full boil and boil hard 2 minutes. Remove from heat; skim off foam, if necessary. Pour hot jelly into hot jars, leaving ¼-inch headspace. Adjust caps.

Process half-pints 5 minutes in a boiling water bath canner.

Yield: about 9 half-pints

Russ Firestone Family, Selah, Washington (Central Washington State Fair, Yakima, Washington)

Jelly-Filled Oat Muffins

MUFFINS

1½ cups all-purpose flour
1 cup quick-cooking rolled oats
1½ teaspoons baking powder
¾ teaspoon baking soda
¼ teaspoon salt
1 teaspoon cinnamon
½ cup brown sugar
¼ cup (½ stick) butter or margarine,
   softened
1 egg
1¼ cups buttermilk
¾ cup raisins
¼ cup Pear Jelly

CRUNCHY TOPPING

3 tablespoons butter or margarine
2 tablespoons brown sugar
½ cup finely chopped walnuts
⅓ cup all-purpose flour

Preheat oven to 375°F. Grease muffin cups; set aside.

To make Muffins: Combine flour, oats, baking powder, soda, salt, and cinnamon in a medium bowl. In a large bowl, combine brown sugar, butter or margarine, and egg; mix well. Add dry ingredients alternately with buttermilk to sugar mixture. Stir in raisins. Pour batter into prepared muffin cups, filling each half full. Spoon 1 teaspoon jelly onto center of each muffin. Carefully spoon remaining batter evenly over jelly to cover.

To make Crunchy Topping: Combine all topping ingredients in a small bowl; using a pastry blender or fork, cut in butter or margarine until mixture resembles coarse crumbs. Sprinkle topping over muffins.

Bake at 375°F for 18 to 25 minutes or until tops are browned and spring back when lightly touched in center. Cool in pan on a wire rack 5 minutes, then remove from pan and continue cooling on rack.

Yield: 12 muffins

Ball Recipe

Plum Jelly

18 pounds fresh plums
1½ cups water
1 package powdered pectin
7½ cups sugar

Prepare home canning jars and lids according to manufacturer's instructions. Jars should be covered with water and boiled 10 to 15 minutes to sterilize.

Wash plums. Combine plums and water in a large pan and bring to a boil; simmer 10 minutes. Place plums in a jelly bag to extract juice.

Measure 5½ cups plum juice into a large saucepan; add pectin and bring to a rolling boil. Add sugar and return to a rolling boil. Boil hard 1 minute, stirring constantly. Remove from heat; skim off foam. Pour hot jelly into hot jars, leaving ¼-inch headspace. Adjust caps.

Process half-pints 5 minutes in a boiling water bath canner.

Yield: about 10 half-pints

Edith Ware, Amarillo, Texas
(Amarillo Tri State Fair, Amarillo, Texas)

Raspberry Jam

2 quarts raspberries, crushed
(about 4 pounds raspberries)
1 package powdered pectin
½ teaspoon butter or margarine
7 cups sugar

Prepare home canning jars and lids according to manufacturer's instructions.

Press crushed raspberries through a strainer lined with three layers of damp cheesecloth. Measure 5 cups raspberry purée into a large saucepan. (If berries do not yield 5 cups purée, add water to make up the difference.) Add pectin and butter or margarine; bring mixture to a full boil over high heat, stirring constantly. Quickly add sugar and return to a full, rolling boil. Boil hard 1 minute, stirring constantly. Remove from heat; skim off foam with a large metal spoon. Pour hot jam into hot jars, leaving ¼-inch headspace. Adjust caps.

Process half-pints 15 minutes in a boiling water bath canner.

Yield: about 5 half-pints

Marie E. Hammers, York, Pennsylvania (York County 4-H Fair, York, Pennsylvania)

Jam-Filled Lattice-Top Coffee Cake

6 cups flour, divided
2 packages instant yeast
½ cup sugar
2 teaspoons salt
1 cup milk
½ cup plus 1 tablespoon water, divided
⅓ cup margarine
2 eggs
2¼ pints (4½ cups) Raspberry Jam
1 egg white
Sugar (optional)

Preheat oven to 350°F.

Combine flour, yeast, sugar, and salt in a large bowl. Heat milk, ½ cup water, and margarine until warm. Add warm liquid to dry ingredients; beat by hand or with mixer until well blended (about 3 minutes). Add eggs and stir until well blended. By hand, stir in enough remaining flour to make a soft dough. Knead dough on a floured surface until smooth and elastic (about 5 to 8 minutes). Place dough in a greased bowl, turning once to grease top. Cover bowl with plastic wrap and let sit in a warm, draft-free place until doubled in bulk (about 1 hour).

Punch dough down and divide into three portions. On a lightly floured surface, roll each portion of dough into a 12x7-inch rectangle. Place each rectangle on a greased cookie sheet. Spread jam lengthwise down the center third of each rectangle (use 1½ cups of jam for each). Cut outside edges of each rectangle into one-inch strips. Starting at either narrow end, fold strips toward center across jam, alternating from side to side. Repeat with remaining rectangles of dough. Beat egg white with 1 tablespoon water and brush over tops of coffee cakes. Sprinkle with sugar, if desired. Cover and let rise in a warm place until almost doubled in bulk (15 to 20 minutes).

Bake at 350°F for 20 to 25 minutes or until golden brown. Remove from baking sheets and cool on racks.

Yield: 3 coffee cakes (1 to eat, 1 to freeze, and 1 to give away!)

NOTE: Choose the jam of your choice—my personal favorites are blueberry, strawberry, or marmalades. This coffee cake freezes well.

*Maureen J. Luczak, Saginaw, Michigan
(Saginaw County Fair, Saginaw, Michigan)*

Rhubarb Jelly

3 pounds rhubarb
1 package powdered pectin
4½ cups sugar

Cut rhubarb into one-inch pieces; chop in a blender or food processor. Extract juice by straining chopped rhubarb in a dampened jelly bag or through several thicknesses of damp cheesecloth for about 2 hours.

Prepare home canning jars and lids according to manufacturer's instructions. Jars should be covered with water and boiled 10 to 15 minutes to sterilize.

Measure 3 cups rhubarb juice into a six- or eight-quart pot; add pectin and bring to a full, rolling boil over high heat, stirring constantly. Add sugar and return to a full, rolling boil. Boil hard 1 minute, stirring constantly. Remove from heat; skim off foam, if necessary. Pour hot jelly into hot jars, leaving ¼-inch headspace. Adjust caps.

Process half-pints 5 minutes in a boiling water bath canner.

Yield: 5 half-pints

Paula Mitchell, Pueblo West, Colorado (Colorado State Fair, Pueblo, Colorado)

Jelly Muffins

2 cups all-purpose or whole-wheat flour
⅓ cup sugar
3 teaspoons baking powder
½ teaspoon salt
1 large egg
¾ cup milk
½ cup vegetable oil
¼ cup Rhubarb Jelly

Preheat oven to 400°F. Grease bottoms only of twelve medium muffin cups; set aside.

Combine flour, sugar, baking powder, and salt. Beat egg, then stir in milk and oil; add to dry ingredients and stir until flour is moistened. (Batter will be lumpy.) Fill muffin cups about half full. Spoon 1 teaspoon jelly onto batter in each cup. Top with enough batter to fill cups about three-fourths full.

Bake at 400°F for about 20 minutes or until golden brown.

Yield: 12 muffins

NOTE: For a surprise, substitute 1 cup cornmeal for 1 cup of the flour.

Paula Mitchell, Pueblo West, Colorado
(Colorado State Fair, Pueblo, Colorado)

Rhubarb Raspberry Jam

1 pint red raspberries (about 1
  pound raspberries)
6 cups sugar
1 cup water
1 cup cooked rhubarb (about ½
  pound rhubarb)

Prepare home canning jars and lids according to manufacturer's instructions.

Wash and drain raspberries. Mash berries; set aside. Combine sugar and water in a saucepan; cook rapidly about 12 minutes. Add raspberries and rhubarb; cook rapidly 10 minutes. Remove from heat; alternately stir and skim off foam for 3 minutes. Pour hot jam into hot jars, leaving ¼-inch headspace. Adjust caps.

Process half-pints 10 minutes in a boiling water bath canner.

Yield: about 6 half-pints

Evelyn R. Meister, Washington, Illinois (Heart of Illinois Fair, Peoria, Illinois)

The Big Cookie

2 cups flour
¾ cup (1½ sticks) butter or margarine
1 cup sugar
1 cup chopped nuts
1 cup flaked coconut
1 cup Rhubarb Raspberry Jam

Preheat oven to 350°F.

Combine flour and butter or margarine in a mixing bowl; using a pastry blender or fork, work together until mixture is crumbly. Add sugar, nuts, and coconut; mix well. Pat half of the crumbly mixture into the bottom of a greased tray or jelly-roll pan. Spread jam gently over top. Spoon remaining crumbly mixture on top of jam and pat gently.

Bake at 350°F for 20 minutes. Cool. Cut into squares to serve.

Yield: 15 servings

NOTE: This is an easy recipe that children can help with.

Marie E. Hammers, York, Pennsylvania
(York County 4-H Fair, York, Pennsylvania)

Rhubarb Peach Jam

1 quart sliced rhubarb (about 1
    pound rhubarb, cut into ¼-
    inch slices)
1½ quarts peeled, pitted and
    crushed peaches (about 3½
    pounds peaches)
⅔ cup water
7 cups sugar
¼ cup lemon juice

Prepare home canning jars and
lids according to manufacturer's
instructions.

Combine rhubarb, peaches, and
water in a large saucepan; cook
gently 10 minutes. Add sugar and
lemon juice; slowly bring to a boil,
stirring until sugar dissolves. Cook
rapidly until thick (about 30
minutes), stirring frequently to
prevent sticking as mixture
thickens. Pour hot jam into hot
jars, leaving ¼-inch headspace.
Adjust caps.

Process pints 15 minutes in a
boiling water bath canner.

Yield: about 4 pints

*John L. Good, Richmond, Kansas
(Kansas State Fair, Hutchinson,
Kansas)*

Jam Good Roll

4 egg yolks
¾ cup sugar, divided
½ teaspoon vanilla
4 egg whites
⅔ cup sifted cake flour
1 teaspoon baking powder
¼ teaspoon salt
Confectioners' sugar
2 cups Rhubarb Peach Jam

Preheat oven to 375°F.

Beat egg yolks until thick and lemon colored; gradually beat in ¼ cup sugar, then add vanilla. Beat egg whites until soft peaks form; gradually add ½ cup sugar and beat until stiff peaks form. Fold egg yolks into egg whites. Sift together flour, baking powder, and salt; fold into egg mixture. Spread batter evenly in a greased and lightly floured 15½x10½x1-inch jelly-roll pan.

Bake at 375°F for 10 to 12 minutes or until done. Immediately loosen sides and turn out cake onto a towel sprinkled with sifted confectioners' sugar. Starting at either narrow end, roll up cake and towel together; cool on a wire rack. Unroll cake and spread with jam. Roll up cake again (without the towel). Cut into one-inch slices to serve.

Yield: 10 slices

John L. Good, Richmond, Kansas (Kansas State Fair, Hutchinson, Kansas)

Serviceberry Jelly

3½ cups serviceberry juice
1 package powdered pectin
4½ cups sugar

Prepare home canning jars and lids according to manufacturer's instructions. Jars should be covered with water and boiled 10 to 15 minutes to sterilize.

Combine juice and pectin in a six- or eight-quart saucepot; bring to a full, rolling boil over high heat, stirring constantly. Add sugar all at once and return to a full, rolling boil (one that cannot be stirred down), stirring constantly. Boil hard 1 minute. Remove from heat; skim off foam, if necessary. Pour hot jelly into hot jars, leaving ¼-inch headspace. Adjust caps.

Process half-pints 5 minutes in a boiling water bath canner.

Yield: about 5 half-pints

NOTE: Serviceberries grow wild in plentiful supply on bushes in the mountain areas of central and western Montana. The berry is approximately ¼ inch in diameter, purplish in color, and has a very mild flavor. The serviceberry is somewhat comparable to the blueberry.

Milly Mathiason, Lewistown, Montana (MontanaFair, Billings, Montana)

Strawberry Preserves

1 heaping quart large-stemmed,
  firm, red strawberries (about
  1¾ pounds strawberries)
3 quarts boiling water
4 cups sugar, divided

Wash and stem strawberries. Place berries in a large kettle and cover with boiling water, then drain in a colander. Return berries to kettle; add 2 cups sugar and mix well. Boil hard 2 minutes. Add remaining 2 cups sugar and boil hard 5 minutes. Pour preserves into a shallow dish. Let stand 24 hours, stirring or shaking frequently.

Prepare home canning jars and lids according to manufacturer's instructions.

Ladle preserves into hot jars, leaving ¼-inch headspace. Adjust caps.

Process half-pints 20 minutes in a boiling water bath canner.

Yield: about 4 half-pints

NOTE: The berries remain whole in this recipe. We spread these preserves on rolls and bread.

*Vyla Blough, Waterloo, Iowa
(National Cattle Congress
Exposition, Waterloo, Iowa)*

Strawberry Coffee Cake

CAKE

1¾ cups flour, divided
1 package dry yeast
¼ cup sugar
½ teaspoon nutmeg
¼ teaspoon salt
⅓ cup milk
⅓ cup water
2 tablespoons shortening
1 egg
½ cup Strawberry Preserves

TOPPING

½ cup flour
½ cup sugar
¼ cup flaked coconut
2 tablespoons butter or margarine, melted
½ teaspoon cinnamon

Preheat oven to 350°F.

To make Cake: Combine 1 cup flour, yeast, sugar, nutmeg, and salt in a large mixing bowl; mix well. Heat milk, water, and shortening in a saucepan until warm (120°F to 130°F). Add hot liquid to flour mixture, then add egg; blend at low speed of electric mixer until moistened, then beat 3 minutes at medium speed. By hand, gradually stir in remaining flour to make a stiff batter. Spread batter in a greased 9 × 9-inch cake pan. Spoon preserves over batter.

To prepare Topping: Combine all ingredients and mix well. Sprinkle topping over preserves. Cover and let rise until doubled in bulk (about 45 minutes).

Bake at 350°F for 30 to 35 minutes or until golden brown. Serve warm.

Yield: 6 to 8 servings

NOTE: You can use apricot preserves in place of the strawberry preserves.

Cindy Tufts, Carmichael, California (California State Fair, Sacramento, California)

Strawberry Rhubarb Jam

2 cups crushed strawberries
   (about 1½ pounds strawberries)
2 cups thinly sliced rhubarb
   (about 1 pound rhubarb)
1 package powdered pectin
5½ cups sugar

Prepare home canning jars and lids according to manufacturer's instructions.

Combine strawberries and rhubarb in a six- or eight-quart pot; add pectin and bring to a full, rolling boil, stirring constantly. Add sugar and return to a full, rolling boil, stirring constantly. Boil hard 1 minute. Remove from heat; skim off foam, if necessary. Pour hot jam into hot jars, leaving ¼-inch headspace. Adjust caps.

Process half-pints 10 minutes in a boiling water bath canner.

Yield: about 7 half-pints

NOTE: If you want a soft set, do not cook the mixture for the full minute after adding sugar.

Genni Piper, Kansas City, Kansas (Wyandotte County Fair, Kansas City, Kansas)

Blushing Angel

1 (16 ounce) angel food cake
1 quart vanilla ice cream
1 cup Strawberry Rhubarb Jam

Cut cake into eight slices. Place one scoop of ice cream on top of each slice of cake. Drizzle 2 tablespoons jam over each scoop of ice cream.

Yield: 8 servings

Genni Piper, Kansas City, Kansas (Wyandotte County Fair, Kansas City, Kansas)

Tomato Marmalade

3 pounds tomatoes
1 orange
½ lemon
3 cups sugar

Wash and peel tomatoes. Cut tomatoes into pieces; cut orange and lemon into thin slices, discarding seeds. Combine all ingredients in a large saucepan; cook mixture slowly for 3 hours, stirring to prevent sticking.

Prepare home canning jars and lids according to manufacturer's instructions.

Pour hot marmalade into hot jars, leaving ¼-inch headspace. Adjust caps.

Process half-pints 15 minutes in a boiling water bath canner.

Yield: about 6 half-pints

Marie A. Lee, Cherry Hill, New Jersey (New Jersey State Fair, Cherry Hill, New Jersey)

CONTRIBUTORS

The individuals listed below are Ball Award winners whose recipes appear in the BALL BLUE-RIBBON COOKBOOK, FIRST EDITION.

Edna Alexander, Harrison, Arkansas; Nicol Alexander, Jonesborough, Tennessee

Marguerite W. Barford, Augusta, West Virginia; Martha Bell, Pryor, Oklahoma; Taffy Benson, Colfax, Wisconsin; Carolyn Bice, Haynesville, Louisiana; Teresa Biggs, Boise, Idaho; Vyla Blough, Waterloo, Iowa; Bonnye Bodiford, Montgomery, Alabama; Louise M. Bodziony, Gladstone, Missouri; Estelle W. Bragg, Vienna, Georgia

Lillian Calhoun, Coushatta, Louisiana; Helen Cameron, Pine Bluff, Arkansas; Carrie Carr, Bluff City, Tennessee; Delmar Case, Fallbrook, California; Rebecca Christensen, Blackfoot, Idaho; Anne E. Cooper, Hayden, Idaho; Alma L. Crawford, Lumpkin, Georgia

Charlene Daniels, Groton, New York; Anna Marie Davis, Fair Oaks, California; Claudia Davis, Hayden Lake, Idaho; Wanda Davis, New Hope, Kentucky; Beulah Devine, Sacramento, Kentucky; Donna Mae Dragseth, Alamo, North Dakota

Paula Faught, New Haven, Kentucky; Gertrude Filipovich, Abilene, Texas; Russ Firestone Family, Selah, Washington

Dorothy Glover, Coushatta, Louisiana; John L. Good, Richmond, Kansas; Cathy Grant, Wasilla, Alaska; Bonnie Groh, East Aurora, New York

Marie E. Hammers, York, Pennsylvania; Lillie Harper, Haynesville, Louisiana; Kaye Heeb, Harrisburg, Arkansas; Rebecca Hoffman, Mesa, Arizona; Gail Marie Holmes-Lee, Bardstown, Kentucky; Eva M. Hudson, Hanna City, Illinois

Patricia E. Jacobs, Pine Bluff, Arkansas; Pauline Jenkins, Bakersfield, California; Deidra Johnson, Riverton, Wyoming; Nancy Johnson, Clever, Missouri

Barbara Kellogg, Coushatta, Louisiana; Dana Kerby, Canyon, Texas; Helen H. Kirsch, Albuquerque, New Mexico; Warren L. Knudtson, Las Vegas, Nevada

Marie A. Lee, Cherry Hill, New Jersey; Alice Like, Murray, Kentucky; Maureen Luczak, Saginaw, Michigan; Carolyn Lynch, Williston, North Dakota; Elizabeth A. Lynch, Boulder, Colorado

Milly Mathiason, Lewistown, Montana; Lynn Matranga, Ontario, California; Evelyn R. Meister, Washington, Illinois; Mildred E. Meyer, Billings, Montana; Thelma Meyer, Bella Vista, California; Nola J. Michael, Laurel, Montana; Elizabeth Miles, Mesa, Arizona; Paula Mitchell, Pueblo West, Colorado; Connie Morgan, Horseshoe Bend, Idaho; Susan C. Moser, King, North Carolina; Debi Mosier, Sperry, Oklahoma; Mrs. Floyd Mounts, Oklahoma City, Oklahoma; Victoria Mowrey, Tampa, Florida; Elinore L. Muccianti, Fresno, California

Scott D. O'Brien, Indianapolis, Indiana; Arleen B. Owen, Fresno, California

Dixie Peterson, Caliente, Nevada; Mary Looker Pfremmer, Smith River, California; Genni Piper, Kansas City, Kansas; Virginia A. Price, Jamesville, New York

Gladys Reisinger, Waterloo, Iowa; Irene Robison, Woodstock, Maryland

Luanne Shafer, Otis, Colorado; Vicki Shook, Wichita, Kansas; Norma I. Souser, Otis, Colorado; Julie Speck, Auburn, New York; Lou Ann Stapp, Columbiana, Alabama; Crystal B. Stewart, Ruston, Louisiana; Terry Swann, Selbyville, Delaware

Lois Tingle, Montevallo, Alabama; Mamie Trefry, Wenatchee, Washington; Cindy Tufts, Carmichael, California; Clarissa Tuor, Santa Rosa, California

Julie Ann Ward, Washington Court House, Ohio; Edith Ware, Amarillo, Texas; Paula G. Webb, Wichita, Kansas; Cynthia Westermier, Arcadia, Oklahoma; Wini Whitaker, Redmond, Oregon; Eugenia Whitlow, Knob Lick, Kentucky; Allison Williams, Scottsdale, Arizona; Madonna Joy Wilson, Fontana, California; Norma Wright, Albuquerque, New Mexico

FAIRS

The fairs listed below are represented in the BALL BLUE-RIBBON COOKBOOK, FIRST EDITION, by recipes from Ball Award winners.

ALABAMA: Alabama State Fair, Birmingham; South Alabama State Fair, Montgomery
ALASKA: Alaska State Fair, Palmer
ARIZONA: Arizona State Fair, Phoenix
ARKANSAS: Northeast Arkansas District Fair, Jonesboro; Northwest Arkansas District Fair, Harrison; Southeast Arkansas District Fair, Pine Bluff
CALIFORNIA: The Big Fresno Fair, Fresno; California State Fair, Sacramento; California State Grange Fair, Sacramento; Del Mar Fair, Del Mar; Kern County Fair, Bakersfield; Los Angeles County Fair, Pomona; Sonoma County Fair, Santa Rosa
COLORADO: Colorado State Fair, Pueblo; Eastern Colorado Round-Up, Akron; Washington County Fair, Akron
DELAWARE: Delaware State Fair, Harrington
FLORIDA: Florida State Fair, Tampa
GEORGIA: Central Georgia Fair, Cordele; Chattahoochee Valley Fair, Columbus
IDAHO: Eastern Idaho State Fair, Blackfoot; North Idaho Fair, Coeur d'Alene; Western Idaho Fair, Boise
ILLINOIS: Heart of Illinois Fair, Peoria
INDIANA: Indiana State Fair, Indianapolis
IOWA: National Cattle Congress Exposition, Waterloo
KANSAS: Kansas State Fair, Hutchinson; Wyandotte County Fair, Kansas City
KENTUCKY: McLean County Fair, Calhoun; Metcalfe County Fair, Edmonton; Murray-Calloway County Fair, Murray; Nelson County Fair, Bardstown
LOUISIANA: Ag Expo 1990, Monroe; Claiborne Parish Fair, Haynesville; Red River Parish Fair, Coushatta

MARYLAND: Maryland State Fair, Timonium
MICHIGAN: Saginaw County Fair, Saginaw
MISSOURI: Missouri State Fair, Sedalia; Ozark Empire Fair, Springfield
MONTANA: MontanaFair, Billings
NEVADA: Las Vegas Jaycees State Fair, Las Vegas
NEW JERSEY: New Jersey State Fair, Cherry Hill
NEW MEXICO: New Mexico State Fair, Albuquerque
NEW YORK: Erie County Fair & Expo, Hamburg; New York State Fair, Syracuse
NORTH CAROLINA: Dixie Classic Fair, Winston-Salem
NORTH DAKOTA: Upper Missouri Valley Fair, Williston
OHIO: Ohio State Fair, Columbus
OKLAHOMA: State Fair of Oklahoma, Oklahoma City; Tulsa State Fair, Tulsa
OREGON: Oregon State Fair, Salem
PENNSYLVANIA: York County 4-H Fair, York
TENNESSEE: Appalachian Fair Association, Gray
TEXAS: Amarillo Tri State Fair, Amarillo; West Texas Fair & Rodeo, Abilene
WASHINGTON: Central Washington State Fair, Yakima; North Central Washington District Fair, Waterville
WEST VIRGINIA: Hampshire County Fair, Augusta
WISCONSIN: Northern Wisconsin State Fair, Chippewa Falls
WYOMING: Wyoming State Fair, Douglas

INDEX

(NOTE: Canned foods are listed in **bold** type; dishes using canned foods as an ingredient are listed in regular type.)

(NOTE: Canned foods are listed in **bold** type; dishes using canned foods as an ingredient are listed in regular type.)

(NOTE: Canned foods are listed in **bold** type; dishes using canned foods as an ingredient are listed in regular type.)

(NOTE: Canned foods are listed in **bold** type; dishes using canned foods as an ingredient are listed in regular type.)

(NOTE: Canned foods are listed in **bold** type; dishes using canned foods as an ingredient are listed in regular type.)

(NOTE: Canned foods are listed in **bold** type; dishes using canned foods as an ingredient are listed in regular type.)